SUCCESSFUL STUDENT TEACHING: A HANDBOOK FOR ELEMENTARY AND SECONDARY STUDENT TEACHERS

By Fillmer Hevener Jr.

C²¹

CENTURY TWENTY ONE PUBLISHING

PUBLISHED BY

CENTURY TWENTY ONE PUBLISHING
POST OFFICE BOX 8
SARATOGA, CALIFORNIA 95070

C₂₁

LIBRARY OF CONGRESS CARD CATALOG NUMBER

80-69332

I.S.B.N.

0-86548-040-0

Copyright 1981

By

Fillmer Hevener, Jr.

PREFACE

A student preparing to teach at either the elementary or secondary level is required to spend a substantial block of time in a real classroom teaching real students real subject matter. This experience -- known as student teaching, interning, or practice teaching -- is challenging to even the most competent and bravest because it is the college student's initial exposure to all the complexities of the profession of teaching. Student teaching is also important because one's fitness to enter the profession is judged largely by the degree of competency displayed during this practicum.

This handbook is a concise, practical, informational guide designed to help steer the college student through the intricacies of student teaching as smoothly as possible. It answers questions often overlooked by those preparing to enter student teaching as well as critical questions frequently asked the author by those already engaged in student teaching. In addition, it suggests specific teaching methods which may be adapted to instructional situations at the elementary and secondary levels.

The exhaustive index adds to the book's practicality as does the orderly, comprehensive inclusion of vital topics in the twelve chapters, three glossaries, and extensive bibliography.

Fillmer Hevener, Jr.

TABLE OF CONTENTS

DEDICATION

I dedicate this book to my dear wife, Celia, my son, Dennis, and my daughter, Yolanda, who gave me their undivided help and encouragement.

CHAPTER 1

A FORWARD LOOK

Various professions require those desiring to become professionals to serve an internship. Teaching is one of these professions. The internship for both elementary and secondary majors is called student teaching, and allows the student teacher, or intern[1], to teach students in an actual classroom setting under professional supervision for a specified period of time, usually eight to ten weeks.

Many college students preparing to teach wonder why they are required to intern. These students often point out that student teaching is not only time consuming, but quite expensive also. Frequently the intern teaches in a school a great distance from the college campus or his home; therefore, he must rent an apartment for some two or three months and in many instances purchase additional clothing as well as provide for his transportation.

1. CONSIDER THE VALUE OF STUDENT TEACHING

Although student teaching is both time consuming and expensive, there are numerous reasons why interning is necessary for those planning to enter the teaching profession. First, the intern is expected to student teach in order to meet state certification requirements. No teacher is allowed to teach on a full-time basis unless he is licensed by the state in which he wishes to teach. In addition, there are two very important personal reasons why he should be exposed to the classroom under professional guidance before assuming a class of his own. The first of these is to find out if he <u>can</u> teach successfully, and the second is to discover if he <u>wants</u> to teach. Spending from eight to ten weeks assuming the full responsibility of a classroom teacher is an expensive and incommodious avenue by which to arrive at answers to these two crucial questions, but there is no other way for most teaching majors to know if they truly wish to enter the teaching profession. Brief pre-student teaching forays into the classroom for the purpose of observing and assisting a teacher can help the teaching major answer these questions, but for most student teachers the final answer comes some time during the student teaching experience.

2. BE PREPARED FOR INSTRUCTIONAL AND HUMAN-RELATIONS CHALLENGES

There are still other reasons for student teaching. When the intern enters the classroom and assumes full responsibility for all activities within its walls, he exposes himself to instructional and human-relations challenges which will severely test his pedagogical skills and his ability to absorb frustrations. For instance, some students are willing, even eager, to learn but lack innate intellectual ability. Other students have superior minds but choose not to use them; the author recalls teaching one creative, intellectual student who did inferior work because she was chronically indolent and unwilling to organize her time.

Morning after morning other students enter class emotionally disconcerted because of a disrupted home environment. Their parents may regularly abuse them and engage in verbal or physical duels at the breakfast table. Many students come to class hungry, and some present themselves unkempt, not having been taught the benefits of personal cleanliness and grooming.

Learn The Students' Problems Early.

As well as being subjected to these types of frustrations, the student teacher meets situations that test his good judgment and ability to control his anger. There is the undisciplined, cocky smart aleck, who regularly orders about fellow students and those teachers who will let him get away with it. There is the timid, frightened student, who is the object of the bullies'

2

jokes and pranks. There is the habitual talker, who seems compelled to chatter from the time he sets foot in the classroom until he walks out the door at the close of class. There is the proverbial joker, constantly engaging in antics and pretentious display in order to be the focus of attention. Finally, there is the gangster, who thrives on extorting food, money, and valuables from other students. Early in student teaching, such problems measure the intern's dedication, objectivity, calmness, and mastery of technique in classroom management.

Be prepared to Work Hard.

Student teaching also tries one's physical stamina. Usually, student teachers are in their classrooms from 8:30 a.m. to 3:30 p.m. During these seven hours, they not only instruct, but may also serve as record keeper, hall and lunchroom monitor, playground supervisor, and disciplinarian. In the evening it is not unusual for the student teacher to spend three to four hours evaluating student papers, developing fresh instructional ideas, preparing instructional materials, reading professional literature, making unit and lesson plans, selecting audio-visual materials, and developing alternate ways to handle Clarence, the class clown and prankster. In addition, it is quite usual for student teachers to have three or four class preparations daily.

Fortunately, the author's student teaching was not so trying as was his first year of full-time teaching. During that first year, he was teaching at both the junior and senior high school levels and daily preparing five different lessons, some of which were not in his major field. Besides this, much of his time and energy went into managing two especially tempermental, restive, and sometimes rowdyish classes. Upon arriving home, the author would discover that his sweet bride had waiting for him a tempting dinner of Pennsylvania Dutch and Southern dishes. However, many times he would be exhausted, unable to eat until he had rested for an hour. Needless to say, he was happy that

3

this schedule did not face him during his student teaching; if it had he might have been turned from a profession which for twenty-six   years has proved to be highly satisfying and rewarding. Student teachers and first-year teachers, especially, must be determined to succeed and be prepared for any eventuality during these early stages of adjustment. Adequate rest, a balanced diet, exercise, and recreation are essential if the student teacher is to keep pace physically with the demanding schedule and maintain a positive mental outlook.

Learn From Professionals.

The intern also gains experience working with professional educators. The principal or assistant principal usually confers with the student teacher as soon as he reports to the school. At this meeting the administrator covers general working policy with which the intern should be acquainted, and the student teacher is given an opportunity to ask questions concerning school policy and regulations.

In addition to conferring with administrators, the student teacher works closely with his supervising teacher, also known as the master teacher or critic teacher. The supervising teacher serves as the intern's constant ad-visor and resource person. Likewise, the student teacher is able to receive professional guidance from the college student teaching counselor,[2] who visits the intern's classroom periodically, evaluating his instructional performance and recommending materials and techniques that will improve his teaching.

Learn To Relate To Parents.

Student teaching provides the intern opportunity to test his ability to work with his students' parents. Parent-Teacher Association meetings and intern-parent conferences afford the student teacher opportunities to learn and to relate to different types of parents, from the supporters to the spoilers.

Learn To Make Wise Instructional Decisions.

Another advantage of student teaching is the occasion it offers the intern to prove his mastery of his area of specialization. The intern, teaching at the elementary or secondary level, attempts to draw upon knowledge and put into practice pedagogical skills learned in the college classroom. After assessing the students' needs and abilities, he chooses the information, materials, and methods of teaching that appear to be instructionally appropriate for his students. Making such selections and applying them to actual teaching-learning situations are among the most challenging pedagogical activities to confront the student teacher.

Learn To Speak Before A Class.

Student teaching permits the intern to test his ability to speak before a group. Unfortunately, many teacher training programs thrust the intern into student teaching without giving him adequate experience in public speaking. Although such lack of experience need not be devastating, the intern should realize that his success in teaching will depend to a large extent upon his ability to develop a pleasant voice, to express his ideas clearly and forcefully, to be calm when standing before his class, and, at the same time, to relate personally to each student in his class. However, if the intern has had little experience in speaking before a group, he will, in most instances and with conscious effort, be able to master satisfactorily these basic speaking skills as he gains teaching experience.

Enjoy Watching Your Students Mature.

Perhaps the most important reason for requiring student teaching is to allow the intern to feel the thrill of seeing his students progress. Nothing is more satisfying to the student teacher than for him to know that he has been able to help his students read with greater acumen, speak with finer precision, and compute with greater accuracy. To help students and daily observe

5

their progress brings the teacher a degree of gratification and fulfillment that few, if any, other professions can offer.

By the end of the student teaching experience, the intern will know if the teaching profession is for him. Happily, the author has discovered that in the vast majority of cases, the intern decides in favor of teaching because, no doubt, he has learned first hand that <u>teaching</u> <u>is</u> <u>giving</u> and that it is "more blessed to give than to receive."[3]

Give Students "Wheat, Not Chaff."

Even though the teacher <u>gives</u>, one may rightfully ask, "<u>What</u> does he give? Chaff or wheat?" The selection which follows will prompt each student teacher to meditate upon this critical question.

I have taught in high school for ten years.
During that time I have given assignments,
among others, to a murderer, an evangelist,
a pugilist, a thief, and an imbecile.

The murderer was a quiet little boy who sat
on the front seat and regarded me with pale
blue eyes; the evangelist, easily the most
popular boy in the class, had the lead in
the junior play; the pugilist lounged by the
window and let loose at intervals a raucous
laugh that startled even the geraniums; the
thief was a gay-hearted Lothario with a song
on his lips; and the imbecile, a soft-eyed
little animal seeking the shadows.

The murderer awaits death in the state penitentiary;
the evangelist has lain a year now in the village
churchyard; the pugilist lost an eye in a brawl in
Hong Kong; the thief, by standing on tiptoe, can see
the windows of my room from the county jail; and the
once gentle-eyed little moron beats his head against
a padded wall in the state asylum.

All of these pupils once sat in my room, sat and
looked at me gravely across worn brown desks. I must
have been a great help to those pupils--I taught them
the rhyming scheme of the Elizabethan sonnet and how
to diagram a complex sentence.

-- N. W. J.[4]

[1]The Terms "student teacher" and "intern" are used interchangeably throughout this book.

[2]For secondary interns, some colleges and universities provide the services of two professionals; one is the education supervisor, representing the department of education, and one the departmental consultant, representing the intern's major department. The education supervisor advises in areas of general educational concern, while the departmental consultant recommends materials and instructional methods appropriate to his particular discipline. For additional discussion of the terms "supervisor," "counselor," and "consultant," see Chapter VIII.

[3]Acts 20:35

[4]Regretfully, the initials N. W. J. are the only signature known to the author of this book.

CHAPTER 2

BECOMING A CANDIDATE FOR STUDENT TEACHING

The student who enrolls in college as an education major may think that anyone planning to teach is automatically considered a candidate for student teaching. Such, however, is not the case.

1. *PREPARE TO BE SCREENED*

When the teaching major is in his second year, many college departments require him to pass a screening test administered by a departmental screening committee.[1] One purpose of the screening committee is to serve as an advisory committee, offering pre-teaching majors professional guidance and counseling as they prepare for student teaching and the teaching profession. A second purpose of the screening committee is to encourage students pursuing the teacher education program to evaluate their own personal objectives, abilities, and interests. Finally, such a committee discourages teaching majors, who demonstrate no real desire or aptitude for teaching, from continuing in the teacher education program.

Become acquainted with screening procedures.

Although screening procedures differ from college to college and department to department, many colleges and departments require that the student declare his intention to become an elementary or secondary teacher by filing an application form with the departmental screening committee sometime during the first half of the sophomore year.

2. *PREPARE TO MAKE FORMAL APPLICATION*

Following is a typical application form to be filled in by the student desiring to become a candidate for student teaching:

Your full name: Date
Your dormitory address:
Your dormitory phone number:
Your home address:
Your home phone number:

---

1. Give the name of one high school teacher who knows you very well:
        Name:
        High School:
        Address:

---

2. Give the name of one college teacher who knows you very well; (If you
   have not completed a course under an instructor at this college, give
   the name of an instructor at another college.)

        Name:
        College:
        Address:

---

3. (a) Name each course you have taken at this college.

        Course   Semester/Year   Teacher of the course

   (b) Please name each of your teachers at this college.

4. (a) (Transfer students) Please name each course you have taken at another
       college.

        Course   Semester/Year   Teacher of the course

   (b) Please name each of your teachers at other colleges.

        Name   College   Address

---

5. What caused you to desire to be a teacher?

---

6. Describe the qualities of your best teacher.

---

7. What do you anticipate to be the least attractive part of being a teacher?

---

8. What do you anticipate to be the <u>most</u> attractive part of being a teacher?

_____

9. (a) What do you see yourself doing in five years?

   (b) What do you see yourself doing in ten years?

   (c) What do you see yourself doing in twenty years?

_____

10. Name any work experience you have had; how long did you hold each position?

_____

11. Name any volunteer work you have performed for your community, church, or school.

_____

12. If you wish to make any additional comments, please use the space below.

_____

Give Additional Information.

After a formal declaration by the student, the screening committee gathers additional information about each student filing a pre-teaching application. Such information generally includes:

1. The cumulative high school grade point average.
2. The cumulative college grade point average.
3. The cumulative college grade point average in the student's major.
4. Academic honors.

5. Non-academic honors.

6. A record of non-academic high school activities.

7. A record of non-academic college activities.

8. Community activities.

9. Scores on selected tests administered to any student whose vocational interest, mental maturity, or emotional stability may be questioned by the screening committee.

Anticipate Being Interviewed.

After gathering and studying information about the education major, the screening committee usually interviews the student for purposes of assisting him in determining his potential for teaching. Students whose potential is questioned may be asked to make several appearances before the committee. The interview usually takes place during the first half of the sophomore year or as soon thereafter as the student declares his intention to become a teaching major. During the interview, normally the student is not evaluated on his mastery of course content since he has been tested on this by his class instructors; however, he is evaluated on his poise, his ability to communicate with clarity and precision, and his general interest in educational matters.

After the interview, the committee makes its report to the departmental faculty and the student, giving reasons for its ultimate recommendation. Each student who is recommended by the screening committee as a candidate for student teaching is normally given a letter of congratulations by the committee. A typical congratulatory letter reads much as the sample which follows:

Dear Student:

Congratulations on your successful interview with the departmental screening committee. Completing this significant step in preparing for teaching is, of course, encouraging. It speaks of your maturity and commitment to a professional purpose.

We wish, however, to offer more than words of reassurance.
It is our privilege to be able to counsel with you, to listen
to your suggestions, to help answer your questions, and to
give direction to your professional program. The committee
looks forward to assisting you in your candidacy for student
teaching.

Cordially,

Chairman
Pre-teaching Committee

3. *REGISTER FOR STUDENT TEACHING.*

After satisfactorily completing the screening test, the teaching major
usually registers for student teaching at the beginning of the second half
of his junior year or the first half of his senior year. The applicant
registers for student teaching as he would for any other course. However,
many colleges require that to this point he have a cumulative grade point
average in all courses of "C" before he is permitted to register for student
teaching.[2] Upon successfully registering for student teaching, the student
is then considered a candidate for the student teaching practicum, but not yet
a student teacher.

4. *STUDY THE COLLEGE'S STUDENT TEACHING HANDBOOK*

Shortly after the candidate has been accepted for student teaching, the
college director of student teaching presents the candidate with a copy of the
college's student teaching handbook, which contains specific information
about that particular college's student teaching practicum.

Typically, a college student teaching handbook touches upon areas such as
the following:

A. The number of clock hours to be spent in observing and in supervised teaching.

B. Procedures followed in assigning student teachers to schools.

C. State certification requirements concerning student teaching.

D. The names of affiliating school divisions.

E. The names of college supervisors and/or consultants.

F. A description of off-campus housing facilities.

G. The intern's relationship to the college while he is student teaching.

H. The intern's relationship to the school in which he is student teaching.

I. Regulations regarding absences of interns from their classes.

J. Suggestions for the supervising teacher.

An early concern of the student teaching candidate should be to digest thoroughly all information in the college's student teaching handbook. Even after a careful study of the handbook, the candidate is likely to have questions, which should be taken to the director of student teaching for clarification.

5. *PREPARE TO BE ASSIGNED TO A SCHOOL*

Soon after the candidate has enrolled in student teaching, the college director of student teaching assigns him to the school where he will serve his internship. This assignment is generally made several months prior to the time the candidate is to begin his student teaching. Normally, the director of student teaching will do his best to place the candidate at a school in the geographic area requested by the candidate. Often, however, the director of student teaching is unable to grant the candidate's request. There may be, for instance, more candidates wishing to student teach in a given school or system than that school or system is prepared to accommodate. At other times the requests of candidates are sometimes rejected because the college does not have

affiliating arrangements with the school system preferred by the candidate.
Be that as it may, if circumstances permit, the candidate should request that
he be placed in a school located near his home so that his expenses for room
and board can be kept to a minimum. If, on the other hand, the candidate
knows that there is no suitable place in his home where he can work in quiet,
he should seriously consider renting his own lodgement while he is serving his
internship. If such should become necessary, the director of student teaching
can assist the intern in arranging for suitable housing and board. Usually,
too, the director is able to assist the intern in arranging for transportation
to and from the school when he does not have his own means of conveyance.

6. *MEET THE SCHOOL ADMINISTRATORS AND SUPERVISING TEACHER AS EARLY AS POSSIBLE*

In addition to providing such assistance, the director of student teaching
normally arranges for the candidate to meet the administrators of the school
at which he will do his internship. Such a meeting usually takes place several
weeks before the candidate is to begin his student teaching. At this meeting
the candidate may expect to receive a handbook for students of the school as
well as a handbook for the school's teachers. The administration outlines the
major responsibilities of the student teacher and gives the candidate opportunity to ask questions.

As well as conferring with the administration, the candidate is also introduced to the classroom teacher who will serve as the candidate's supervising
teacher during the period of internship. After meeting the supervising
teacher, the candidate may then observe one or more of the school's classes.
In many instances these classes will be, and if possible should be, the same
ones which the candidate will teach during his internship.

After the teaching major has passed his screening test, reached the appropriate grade point average, enrolled in student teaching, and visited the
school where he will intern, he is then "promoted", formally or informally,

15

from the status of a candidate for student teaching to that of a full-fledge

student teacher.

[1] In some college departments, screening committees are referred to as pre-teaching committees.

[2] Check the college catalogue for the specific requirements at your college; some colleges require the student to have a grade point average of "C" in his major before he can register for student teaching.

CHAPTER 3

LEARNING THE COMMUNITY AND SCHOOL

A week or ten days before the intern is to begin student teaching, it is advisable for him to move from the college campus to the quarters where he will live during his internship. Although for some this is likely to mean added expense, an early move gives the student teacher opportunity to settle in, unpack, adjust to his new home, and begin learning the community if he is not already acquainted with it.

1. MEET THE COMMUNITY

Becoming familiar with the community pays off handsomely. When meeting the landlord, neighbors, merchants, and others in the normal course of moving into a new community, especially a small community, the student teacher is beginning to establish community relations.

Make Positive Impressions Early.

It is important that the intern's early impressions on the community be positive because the first impressions one makes on another tend to be permanent. Therefore, the student teacher who is initially viewed by the community as alert, congenial, and dedicated is beginning with a decided advantage. Although the intern may be able to meet personally only a dozen citizens during this "settling-in" period, word-of-mouth is still a rapid means of communication, and those initial impressions left with others will be translated into words of commendation or censure as they make their way from person to person in the community.

Work For Smooth Community Relations.

The intern should nurture these initial positive impressions, of course, by doing his best to make for smooth community relations throughout his entire student teaching experience. Such a relationship is likely to be sustained when the student teacher shows that he wishes to become an active, contributing member of the community. Although his time is limited, he may wish to participate in local church functions, scouting activities, volunteer welfare organizations, or other such beneficient groups.

Learn The Social And Economic Composition Of The Community.

So that the student teacher will be in a position to anticipate some of the needs and interests of the students he will be teaching, he should also become familiar with the social and economic composition of the community before he begins teaching. Students from the inner city are likely to have needs and interests somewhat different from those of suburbia, and those from the highlands and mountains will have interests and concerns somewhat unlike those from the more progressive, mechanized rural areas. The student teacher who is sensitive can learn much about the social make-up of the school district if he will keep keen eyes and ears as he talks with others and makes routine trips to such places as the super market, the restaurant, the bank, and the laundry. If a student teacher has his own transportation, it is advisable for him to take several drives through the school district for the purpose of gathering as much information and as many impressions as possible through careful observation. Besides receiving impressions of the quality of housing and the general range and level of the economic prosperity of the citizens, the student teacher can also evaluate the community's recreational and cultural facilities outside the school. The number of parks, libraries, museums, churches, and synagogues suggests the level of economic prosperity as well as the educational, cultural, and spiritual concerns of the citizens of the school district.

2. *SCHEDULE A PRE-TEACHING CONFERENCE*

After meeting citizens of the community and acquainting himself with both the needs and resources of the school district, the student teacher then plans to learn as much as possible about the school where he will student teach before his classroom teaching actually begins. Perhaps the most efficient way to do this is by a pre-teaching conference. The intern makes an appointment with the supervising teacher, who is, in most instances, pleased to set up a conference and happy that the intern is demonstrating enthusiasm by doing a substantial amount of preparation before he enters the classroom to observe and teach.

Learn The Bell Schedule.

The purpose of this pre-teaching conference is to give the student teacher opportunity to gather information. Together, the intern and supervising teacher should study a copy of the bell schedule, noting any irregularities such as split periods or special times for pep rallies and assemblies. If the college director of student teaching has not, prior to this conference, provided a bell schedule, the intern should obtain a copy from his supervising teacher or the school secretary in the administrative office.

Learn Referral Procedures.

From time to time, the student teacher may need to refer insubordinate students to the administrative office. Instead of waiting until a crisis arises in the classroom, the intern should become acquainted early with referral procedures. This initial conference offers the intern opportunity to discuss referral procedures with the supervising teacher. Each school has its own procedures that teachers are to follow when referring a student to the central office. Many administrators ask the teacher to accompany the student to the office; some administrators ask the teacher to send them the student and explain at the end of the class period why the student was referred to the administration. In some schools where two-way electronic voice communication exists between the classroom and the central office, the teacher is asked to "call in" a verbal explanation to the administrator before the student is sent to the office. Be that as it may, the beginning intern needs to have clearly in mind the referral procedures used in his school.

Learn Routine Non-Teaching Responsibilities.

The pre-teaching conference also gives the student teacher occasion to learn what his routine, non-teaching responsibilities will be. The supervising teacher can inform the intern of supervisory responsibilities he may have during lunch periods, home room periods, and assemblies. In addition, some administrators ask that student teachers assist in patrolling playgrounds at specific times, usually immediately before and after school as well as during recess. Frequently, student teachers also assist in watching the hallways before and after school, during recess, and while classes change.

Learn When Faculty And Departmental Meetings Are Held.

When counseling with the supervising teacher at the pre-teaching conference, the intern should also ask for information about faculty meetings and departmental meetings. Faculty meetings are generally held after school hours at least once each month for the purpose of discussing academic, social, and administrative problems of the school. Although these meetings are called by the administration, the faculty is generally encouraged to submit items for the agenda and participate fully in identifying, analyzing, and seeking solutions to problems confronting the school. Much like general faculty meetings, departmental meetings at the secondary level are usually scheduled monthly and offer members of a given department opportunity to discuss topics of departmental concern. The student teacher should attend faculty and departmental meetings and participate in the discussions; however, because of his limited experience in educational matters, he should make suggestions with deliberate caution and discretion. The intern will gain most from faculty and departmental meetings when he determines to learn by listening rather than by telling.

21

Ask About The Availability Of Instructional Materials.

The pre-teaching conference also gives the student teacher opportunity to ask questions about the availability of such instructional materials as film-strips, 16mm films, learning tapes, slides, reading machines, and programmed texts. The intern should also become informed concerning procedures to be followed when reserving and ordering these materials.

When In Doubt, Ask Questions.

At this conference, the student teacher will want to ask about such essential matters as the time when he is to be in his classroom each morning, when he may leave in the afternoon, and the procedures to follow if a student should become ill in class or if the intern, himself, would need to be absent. The intern should not feel that any of his questions is unimportant; a rule to follow is: when in doubt about what to do or how to do it, ask the supervising teacher, who will either answer the question or direct the intern to a source that can give an answer.

3. BECOME ACQUAINTED WITH THE LIBRARY'S FACILITIES

While the student teacher is visiting the school for the pre-teaching conference, it is advisable for him to meet the librarian and become acquainted with the library's facilities since the library is a storehouse of knowledge for both teacher and pupil. The intern should review the fiction, non-fiction, reference, media, newspaper, and periodical holdings. He should also acquaint himself with the classification system used by the librarian. While most larger schools have adopted either the Library of Congress classification or the Dewey Decimal system of classification, some libraries in smaller schools have developed their own systems which they feel best fits their students' needs. The student teacher should also acquaint himself with the location of the card catalogue and such frequently used indexes to periodicals as: Poole's Index, Reader's Guide, Book Review Digest, International Index, and the New

York Times Index. Likewise, the intern may wish to learn the location of such special indexes to periodicals as: the Art Index, Biography Index, Dramatic Index, Education Index, Industrial Arts Index, Music Index, and Technical Review Index. The student teacher may also wish to acquaint himself with the location of such library holdings as: Biological Abstracts, Chemical Abstracts, and Psychological Abstracts as well as general unabridged dictionaries, special dictionaries (e.g. Horwill's Dictionary of Modern American Usage), general encyclopedias, special encyclopedias (e.g. Encyclopedia of Educational Research), atlases and gazetteers, yearbooks (e.g. Information Please Almanac), biographical dictionaries, and literary dictionaries (e.g. Harper's Dictionary of Classical Literature and Antiquities).

The intern who becomes acquainted early with the community and school is likely to enter the classroom informed, well adjusted, and confident.

CHAPTER 4

KEEPING FIT

After the student teacher has acquainted himself with the community and school, he should begin planning how he will budget his time and maintain good health during his internship.

1. BE AWARE THAT TEACHING IS DEMANDING

Before beginning actual instruction, some student teachers think that teaching is not a demanding profession. When assuming instructional responsibilities, however, the student teacher will discover that such a notion is without foundation. A bit of simple arithmetic shows clearly that teaching absorbs an <u>enormous</u> amount of <u>time</u>, and this <u>time</u>, in turn, absorbs <u>vast</u> amounts of <u>energy</u>. The analysis which follows is an estimate of the average amount of time spent each day by a dedicated elementary or secondary teacher:

		Hours	Minutes
a.	Teaching each day.	6	
b.	Supervising a classroom thirty minutes before classes begin and thirty minutes after classes end	1	
c.	Preparing for classes	2	
d.	Evaluating papers	2	
e.	Keeping classroom and school records		30
f.	Doing professional reading	1	30
g.	Attending faculty and committee meetings		30
h.	Doing professional writing		30
i.	Serving as sponsor to a student group		12
j.	Conferring with students and parents "after hours"		12
		12	14 4
	(or)		
		14 hours	24 min.

24

Therefore, the total estimated average amount of work time spent <u>each</u> <u>day</u> by the dedicated professional elementary or secondary teacher is well over fourteen hours, and the student teacher may expect to spend approximately the same number of hours each day in work time.

In order to determine the estimated average amount of time spent <u>each</u> <u>week</u> by the professional teacher, multiply 14 hours and 24 minutes by five days per week; this amounts to an astonishing 72 hours per week! Although the intern's hours may not always be so many, he will, however, spend very long hours, too; therefore, the student teacher needs to give special attention to budgeting his time and guarding his health.

Make a time chart.

What is the best way for the intern to be sure that he will have enough time to care for the numerous responsibilities that he must assume? Perhaps the student teacher can approach this problem most effectively by drawing up a time-chart showing what he is to be doing each hour of the school day. The ensuing time chart may serve as a general model; nevertheless, the student teacher will need to make necessary adjustments to bring the chart into line with his individual needs.

AM
_____

7:00-8:00	Rise, shower, dress
8:00-9:00	Breakfast; ride or walk to school; organize teaching materials
9:00-10:00	Teaching
10:00-11:00	Teaching
11:00-12:00	Teaching

PM
_____

| 12:00-1:00 | Lunch; monitor hallways, classroom, playground |

1:00-2:00	Teaching
2:00-3:00	Teaching
3:00-4:00	Monitor hallways, playground, classroom; drive or walk home
4:00-5:00	Relax, bathe, put on casual clothing
5:00-6:00	Prepare dinner, eat
6:00-7:00	Evaluate papers
7:00-8:00	Evaluate papers, do professional reading
8:00-9:00	Prepare for classes
9:00-10:00	Prepare for classes; prepare to retire
10:00pm-7:00am	Sleep

Notice that this suggested time chart recommends nine hours of sleep! Because of the new and heavy schedule, the intern should get an abundance of rest or he is likely to have poor posture, be mentally dull, drowsy, irritable, grouchy, and hard to please.

2. *KEEP NERVOUS ENERGY IN RESERVE*

People, of course, have different amounts of nervous energy. Some become easily fatigued by a minimum of work while others appear to be able to keep going at a rapid pace with a minimum of rest. The important principle to keep in mind is that every intern does have an exhaustible supply of nervous energy, which is used during the teaching day, and unless this supply of energy is replaced by an adequate amount of sleep, trouble lurks ahead.

Get Adequate Sleep.

Some student teachers may be able to get along on seven hours of sleep; others may require eight, and still others will demand nine. A good rule-of-thumb for the intern to follow is to schedule the day so that he provides for an hour of sleep beyond what he thinks he needs. This extra hour allows for those times when it is impossible to get to bed on time or when he finds

26

falling asleep difficult.

Remember, to a great extent, the success of a student teacher depends on his ability to conserve his energy by allowing adequate time for sleep, for it is during sleep that he restores the energy which he used the previous day. *Allow The Mind To Rest.*

Also, leave weekends open. The mind needs rest and the body requires exercise and fresh air. For variety the intern should engage in activities other than those carried on during the week. He should use the weekends to re-fresh himself spiritually, physically, and mentally. This can be done by be-coming involved in such activities as worshipping God, meditating, hiking, reading and writing for enjoyment, playing physically exerting games, being with friends, and traveling. Except in emergencies, the student teacher should plan weekend activities that take him away from grading papers, planning les-sons, and preparing teaching materials. Weekends must be a special time to which the intern can look forward with relish.

3. EAT A BALANCED DIET

As well as arranging for adequate rest and relaxation, the intern also needs to give attention to eating a balanced diet. A satisfactory diet is one which allows the student teacher to meet his daily demands and be free from illness while enjoying physical fitness and good health.

How much food should be eaten each day? Although the amount required will vary from person to person, the average person needs about three and a half ounces of protein, three and a half ounces of fat, and four ounces of car-bohydrates. Proteins are contained chiefly in beans, fish, meat, eggs, milk, cheese, and peas. Fats are present in butter, milk, some varieties of fish, olive oil, nuts, and margarine. Carbohydrates include such foods as bread, cereals, sugar, potatoes, bananas, dates, raisins, and figs.

Roughage, which is also needed in the diet, is provided in fruits, vegetables, and the bran of cereals. Especially good roughage foods are oatmeal, whole-wheat bread, salads, prunes, cabbage, and apples.

There are two simple, but important dietary principles for the student teacher to remember. The first is to follow the ancient maxim, "Eat breakfast like a king, dinner like a prince, and supper like a pauper." The second is _moderation_ and _variety_. _Abstain_ from anything that is harmful; enjoy a moderate amount of that which is beneficial. Following these simple guidelines will help keep the intern physically fit, mentally alert, and happy.

4. AVOID SMOKING

Unless one is healthy, he cannot, of course, experience full happiness in his profession. Proper habits should be formed early, and the intern needs to be aware of the physical dangers involved in smoking.

Although the dangers may not always be obvious immediately, they will rear their heads in later life. Remember, tabacco is habit forming, and its effect on the body reaches the internal substance of each cell to bring about protoplasmic poisoning. The central substance of each cell is drugged; this, in turn, endangers the very life of the cell. The stomach, as well as the nervous system, is thrown out of balance. Frequently nicotine, found in tobacco, causes the stomach to be susceptible to ulcers. Smoking, by restricting blood circulation, brings on circulatory diseases and promotes chronic bronchitis, emphysema, and strokes.[1]

5. AVOID ALCOHOL

Like tobacco, alcohol interrupts the normal functions of a healthy mind and body. Contrary to popular belief, alcohol acts primarily as a depressant, not as a stimulant. It puts to sleep man's higher brain centers where his reason, will power, and judgment reside. With these centers depressed, man's brain is similar to that of an animal. His good sense and self-discipline are gone. He thinks he is stronger, but he is weaker; he thinks he is more brilli-

28

ant, but he is less so; he feels better physically, but he is worse. Also, like tobacco, alcohol is a drug that attacks the protoplasmic cells. It encourages stomach and liver problems and is, of course, habit forming. There is a clear relationship between the mind and body. The mind may be expected to function best when the body is operating at peak efficiency.

6. DEMONSTRATE SELF CONTROL

The intern who wishes to overcome the tobacco and alcohol habit will find the following rules of Dr. J. Wayne McFarland, trying, but helpful:

1. Whenever one craves a smoke or drink, take slow, deep breaths. Inhale slowly and exhale slowly. Resolve, "I <u>choose</u> not to smoke; I <u>choose</u> not to drink."

2. Take a warm bath in a full tub twice each day. Relax and drink a couple glasses of steaming lemonade while resting in the tub.

3. Drink at least eight glasses of water between meals each day. Remember, 74.5% of the brain and 83% of the blood is water; at this time the body needs to flush away the accumulated poisons.

4. After each meal, take a brisk fifteen to thirty minute walk.

5. When you feel as though you must have a smoke or drink, take another warm bath or shower.

6. Avoid mustard, spices, vinegar, pepper, catsup, rich desserts, and fried foods.

7. <u>Abstain</u> from fish, meat, <u>tea</u>, <u>coffee</u>, and cola drinks.

8. Eat plenty of vegetables, fruit, nuts, cereals, milk, and margarine.

9. For an abundance of vitamins, especially B complex, at each meal eat at least two tablespoonfuls of wheat germ.

10. Ask God to help you break the habit. Pray for power.[2]

The student teacher may obtain additional help from: Narcotics Education, Inc., 6840 Eastern Avenue, N. W., Washington, D. C. 20012.

[1]J. Wayne McFarland, M.D. Better Living. (Washington, D. C.: Review and Herald Publishing Association, 1973), 58, 59.

[2]Ibid., pp. 59-61.

CHAPTER 5

ORGANIZING FOR TEACHING

After planning a balanced time schedule providing for work, adequate sleep, exercise, and recreation, the intern should then turn his attention to organizing the basic teaching materials he will use during his student teaching.

1. HAVE SUPPORTING MATERIALS AVAILABLE

In addition to having access to key reference materials noted in Chapter 3, the intern should take with him his relevant college notes and class handouts, especially those collected in his teaching methods classes. College textbooks and bibliographies should also be readily available for purposes of information and reference.

Be Familiar With Selected Books.

Also, the student teacher will find the following selected books helpful in dealing with routine teaching situations as well as unexpected problems arising in the classroom:

Bremar, John, and Moschizesker, Michael. The School Without Walls.

Brubacher, John S. A History of the Problems of Education.

Combs, A. W., Avila, D. L., and Purley, W. W. Helping Relationships.

Dreeben, Robert. The Nature of Teaching: Schools and the Work of Teachers.

Evans, William H. The Creative Teacher.

Ginott, H. G. Group Psychotherapy With Children.

Gorman, Alfred H. Teachers and Learners: The Interactive Process in Education.

Holt, J. The Underachieving School.

Hoover, Kenneth H. Learning and Teaching in the Secondary School.

Kounin, J. S. Discipline and Group Management in Classrooms.

Silberman, C. E. Crisis in the Classroom.

Be familiar with selected journals.

In order to stay abreast of current teaching methods, research, and trends in education, the student teacher should have access to basic educational journals.

Most school, college, university, and larger city libraries subscribe to many of the following professional magazines:

(1) General. Education Digest, Education Summary, Harvard Educational Review, Teachers College Record, Educational Studies, and Peabody Journal of Education.

(2) Elementary and Secondary Education.

   A. General. Grade Teacher, Instructor, Clearing House, Today's Education, PTA Magazine, and Elementary School Journal.

   B. Disciplines. Agricultural Education Magazine, Art Education, Business Education Forum, Classical Journal, Counselor Education and Supervision, Dramatics, Journal of Industrial Arts Education, The Mathematics Teacher, Media and Methods, Scholastic Coach, Sociology of Education, Technical Education News, Elementary English, English Journal, Journal of Reading, The Reading Teacher, School Science and Mathematics, and School Shop.

Although few interns find time to read as many professional journals as they would like, every intern should read regularly several that are directed especially to his specific teaching interest.

Develop an "Idea File."

As well as having available primary reading materials, every student pre-

32

paring to teach should develop an "idea file," an organized collection of fresh instructional ideas that may be used to stimulate and sustain interest in the subject matter being taught. Fortunate is the beginning student teacher whose college methods teacher required that an "idea file" be developed. However, if the student is facing student teaching without the instructional support which an "idea file" can offer, he should begin immediately to build such a file. Although it is beyond the scope of this book to explain how to develop an "idea file" for each elementary grade and in all disciplines at the secondary level, perhaps a brief explanation of how to go about building such a file would be helpful.

Suppose, for instance, that the college student preparing to teach high school English, wishes to develop an "idea file." First, he should list the areas in which he may be teaching. Then he should provide a means for keeping an accurate record of the number of instructional ideas collected under each heading in the discipline of English. Perhaps the most convenient way to do this is by a chart such as the one which follows:

INSTRUCTIONAL AREAS	NUMBER OF ENTRIES	NOTES AND COMMENTS
Book Reports		
Bulletin Boards		
Creative Writing		
Drama		
Expository Writing		
Games		
Grammar		
Language		
Library		
Listening		

INSTRUCTIONAL AREAS	NUMBER OF ENTRIES	NOTES AND COMMENTS
Mass Media (Electronic)		
Mythology		
Novel		
Poetry		
Punctuation and Mechanics		
Questioning Methods in Literature and Language		
Reading		
Short Story		
Slow Learners		
Speech		
Spelling		
Teaching Resources		
Theme Reading (Evaluation)		
Vocabulary Building		
Other		

The next step is to purchase a 3"x5" file box and a package of 3"x5" file cards. After doing this, the student is then ready to begin searching for fresh instructional ideas. Many such ideas may be found in college notes, in teaching methods books and journals as well as pamphlets and reports published by professional teaching organizations. The student may also wish to include effective instructional methods used by elementary, high school, and college teachers whom he has observed.

Develop a "Materials File."

In addition to an "idea file," each student teacher should have available a "materials file." The "materials file" allows the intern to organize and have accessible materials which he will (or may) need to support his instruction during his student teaching. The specific kinds of materials to be collected and filed depend on the grades and subjects being taught. Generally, however, the "materials file" should include such items as: film, filmstrip, disc record, cassette tape, and laboratory equipment catalogues. The file should also include appropriate 2"x2" slides, graphs, posters, pictures and games. "Cut-outs" should be included for two or three bulletin boards that will relate to the grade level and subject being taught during student teaching. In addition, the intern should collect a wide variety of pictures that may be used for decorating the classroom or for adding a visual dimension to teaching when such is instructionally appropriate.

Copies of student-oriented newspapers, magazines, and books should be included in the "materials file." Companies such as Xerox, Scholastic, and Reader's Digest publish these materials and normally offer free sample copies to interested teachers and student teachers.

Use 16mm Films.

Student teachers may order instructional 16mm films from the film library of the state, county, or city system in which he is teaching. Films are being used more and more as effective supportive instructional tools. Since it is not unusual for certain popular films to be booked for several weeks in advance, the intern should book all films as early as possible.

Seek Assistance Whenever Necessary.

If at any time the student teacher discovers that he cannot find necessary instructional materials, he should not hesitate to seek assistance from his supervising teacher, his college supervisor or consultant, and the school's media resource person.

Although preparing and organizing one's materials in advance takes considerable time and effort, such planning makes for a confident, well-prepared student teacher.

CHAPTER 6

YOUR FIRST DAYS AS A STUDENT TEACHER

Teaching is a demanding profession at all times; however, perhaps at no time is it so demanding as it is during student teaching. First, the intern is inexperienced and, therefore, likely to be apprehensive. Working under such apprehension places added strain on him. Second, the intern must go into a classroom situation that has, for the most part, already been structured by the supervising teacher. Even though the supervising teacher may have set a classroom climate conducive to learning, the student teacher may find that fitting into a previously jelled classroom milieu can be awkward.

1. *ADJUST TO STUDENT TEACHING EARLY*

Be that as it may, the intern should be aware that student teaching is a trial period and that success as an intern is essential if he is to become a professional educator. Beyond doubt, the most crucial segment of the student teaching experience is the first few days. The student teacher who cannot adjust, getting off to a poor start, is more likely to encounter serious trouble later than is the student teacher who, from the first day, adjusts to the new teaching situation.

Be Flexible.

In order to make a smooth entry into teaching, the intern needs to demonstrate a great measure of flexibility, giving here and taking there, as the situation demands.

Be Open To Suggestions And Seek Assistance.

Although the student teacher needs to be <u>willing</u> at all times to receive advice from the supervising teacher and the college supervisor, at no time is such willingness as essential as it is during the early day of student teaching. The student teacher should always _feel_ _free_ to seek help from his supervisors, who are by his side for the express purpose of doing all they can to see that the intern's student teaching experience is successful and, being such, a triumphal entry into the profession of teaching.

2. *MAINTAIN A POSITIVE SELF-IMAGE*

From the very outset, the intern should adopt a positive attitude toward himself. As the ancient Athenian philosopher, Socrates, recommended some five hundred years before Christ, every man should daily examine himself in order that he might know himself.

Before one can expect to understand others, he should know himself. So it is with the student teacher. Before he can expect to understand his students, he should examine and attempt to understand himself. Being as objective as possible, the intern needs to recognize both his pedagogical weaknesses and strengths. He may broaden and sharpen his view of his teaching by requesting, for the first few days, especially, evaluations by his supervising teacher.

Eliminate Weaknesses.

Although the intern should recognize and accept his shortcomings, he should, at the same time, with assistance from his supervising teacher and college supervisor, carry out plans to eliminate these weaknesses. Also, the intern must not become discouraged should he realize that he is not as telling in his teaching as other more experienced professionals. Even though the trite adage "practice makes perfect" may be only partially true and not always applicable, in teaching, practice does make for improvement even though within a teacher's lifetime "perfection" may never be achieved. Therefore, during the early days of student teaching, especially, the intern should view himself positively, realizing that he is in the process of embarking upon a profession in which his pedagogic skills will become more refined with experience.

37

Show Enthusiasm For Learning.

In addition to having a positive attitude toward himself from the very first class period, the student teacher should display sincere enthusiasm for learning. If the students detect a careless attitude by the intern toward the subject he is teaching, they are likely to conclude that if the intern cannot find joy in learning, why should they expect to find learning a rewarding, enjoyable experience. Students with such a frame of mind are not likely to be motivated or possess a spirit of inquiry. Therefore, if the student teacher is to motivate his students, it is vital that he, himself, show esprit de corps for learning.

In short, the beginning student teacher should be critical and patient with himself, flexible, enthusiastic, and self-confident, yet modest and unassuming.

3. *BECOME FAMILIAR WITH THE SCHOOL*

If the intern has not had opportunity to acquaint himself with the school's buildings beforehand, during the first few days of student teaching, he should learn the names of the buildings, the number pattern of classrooms, and the location of the library, the auditorium, the clinic, and the emergency exits of the building in which he is to teach.

Organize Materials.

On the first day of his student teaching, the intern should familiarize himself with the class schedule so that he may have his instructional materials organized and ready for immediate use at the beginning of each class. Nothing frustrates the intern more than knowing that his teaching materials for the next class are "somewhere" in his room, but not knowing where he can find them during the limited time available between classes. Such organization is absolutely necessary for the secondary student teacher, especially, since often he must gather his materials and walk across campus to another building within the ten minutes normally allowed for class change.

Be Punctual.

From the beginning the intern should be punctual. Being accountable for homeroom, lunchroom, and hall supervision, as well as teaching responsibilities, the intern needs to be on time for every appointment. The watchful eye of the student teacher can keep calm and order among students who, otherwise, could become uproarious and disorderly during the change of classes and the early minutes of a class period. The intern who is habitually late also tends to lose the respect of the students, the supervising teacher, and the college counselor, for these people conclude that the intern who cannot discipline himself to be punctual can neither discipline himself to prepare well for his instructional responsibilities in the classroom.

4. *BE ACCESSIBLE TO PARENTS AND STUDENTS*

As soon as the intern begins teaching, he should make clear to his students and their parents that he is available for private conferences at specified hours and at other times by appointment. Although the intern will have some opportunity to counsel students in class, the public nature of a classroom setting does not encourage students to discuss problems of a personal nature. Many teachers find that being available for conferences for an hour after school once or twice a week promotes good will and understanding between the students and the teacher as well as the parents and the teacher.

5. *MAKE A GOOD APPEARANCE*

From the first day, the student teacher wants to make a positive impression on his students. In addition to being organized, demonstrating a command of his discipline, and knowing how to create an atmosphere conducive to learning, the intern wants to make a good appearance. The male student teacher desires to be neat as a nail, while the female student teacher wants to be fresh as a flower. Both should form the habit of daily caring for such routine personal matters as: applying deodorant or antiperspirant; bathing for relaxation and cleansing; trimming, brushing, and combing the hair; cleaning and filing the fingernails; soaking the feet, clipping the nails, and filing for smoothness; and applying a fragrance that fits the wearer's personality, his individual body chemistry, and the occasion, teaching.

Show Good Taste In Dress.

In addition to being well groomed, the intern desires to display good taste in dress. Although good taste is difficult to define, most fashion experts agree that it includes wearing clothes that are in keeping with the occasion, that are not gaudy, but that are delightfully comfortable and well coordinated.

Avoiding extreme styles, the intern should, therefore, dress so as to be attractive and smart, for his appearance suggests how he views himself professionally. Just as carefulness and taste in dress imply professional concern and competence, so carelessness and slovenliness suggest professional indifference and incompetence.

6. BE A KEEN OBSERVER

For the first day or two, the supervising teacher usually allows the student teacher to observe the students he will be teaching before he begins to assume instructional responsibilities. During this time of adjustment, the intern should be a keen observer, marking how the supervising teacher handles such routine classroom matters as adjusting the windows for proper ventilation, the blinds for adequate light, and the thermostat for a comfortable temperature. The intern should also take careful note of classroom rules and how the supervising teacher handles the implementation of these rules.

Learn Students' Names.

As soon as the student teacher is introduced to each class, he should begin learning the names and seating positions of all students. An efficient

Teacher's
Desk

	Column 1	Column 2	Column 3	Column 4	Column 5	Column 6	Column 7	Column 8
Row 1	Joe Brown	Merle Troyer	Sally Sites	Gerald Gaines	Bud Holbert	Mary Maize	Hilda Homber	Rose Redd
Row 2	Betty Ayers		Gary Sykes	Ellen Evendon		Bill Stewart	Mossey Morris	
Row 3		Happy Herald	Celia Centron		Tammy Bellowe		Cindy Kerns	Joe Oakes
Row 4	Allie Arnold	Marcia Greco		Tom Gaines	Phil Fowler	Floyd Aiken	Humber Hanks	Dennis Dykes
Row 5								

41

way to do this is through the use of a seating chart such as the sample on the previous page.

As can be seen, the above chart represents a somewhat formal, traditional seating arrangement with the desks placed in rows and columns. This chart indicates that there are twenty-five students seated in the classroom, which can seat forty. The blank blocks on the chart represent desks not in use.

If the student teacher wishes to design a seating chart representative of a more informal, modern semicircular seating arrangement, a chart such as the following may be used.

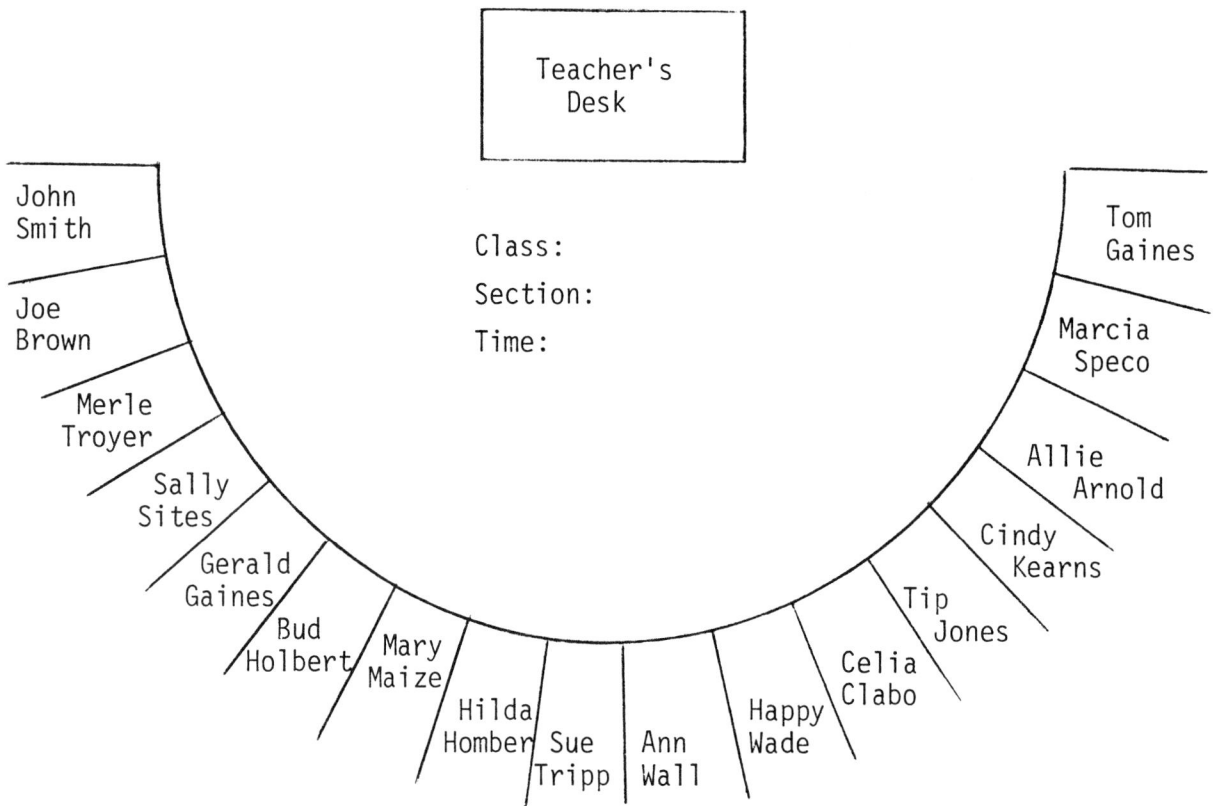

Teacher's
Desk

Class:

Section:

Time:

John
Smith

Joe
Brown

Merle
Troyer

Sally
Sites

Gerald
Gaines

Bud
Holbert

Mary
Maize

Hilda
Homber

Sue
Tripp

Ann
Wall

Happy
Wade

Celia
Clabo

Tip
Jones

Cindy
Kearns

Allie
Arnold

Marcia
Speco

Tom
Gaines

Should it be desirable ultimately to allow the students to sit where they wish each period, assigning seats for a couple of weeks allows the intern to learn the names of the students before they are permitted to choose desks at random.

7. *NOTE STUDENT INVOLVEMENT*

Not only should the student teacher make an early, conscious effort to learn the names of each student, but he should also observe the degree of involvement of each student in learning activities. For instance, a lack of involvement on the part of a student suggests that he may have learning difficulties which the instructor would want to explore. On the other hand, a student enthusiastically involved in learning activities challenges the teacher to direct such fervor into productive channels of learning.

8. *BECOME ACQUAINTED WITH LEARNING MATERIALS*

During the first few days of observing, and earlier if at all possible, the intern should acquaint himself thoroughly with all formal textbooks and learning materials to be used in his classes, for it is to these learning tools, especially, that he will direct the attention of his students throughout his student teaching experience. He will also need to consider the selection of extra teaching supplies that will support the formal materials and assist him in individualizing instruction and reaching the instructional objectives set for his classes.

9. *CAREFULLY OBSERVE SUPERVISING TEACHER*

During this period of adjustment, the student teacher should carefully observe the instructional style of the supervising teacher. Although the intern will want to "be himself" and discover the approaches and methods that are best for him, he is likely to find that the supervising teacher employs some teaching techniques which will fit well into his own instructional style.

After observing the supervising teacher for several days, the intern usually finds that he can hardly wait to begin teaching. His impatience

mounts! This impatience, sparked by his enthusiasm, prepares him for that

memorable day when the supervising teacher will give him his very own class.

CHAPTER 7

RELATING TO THE SUPERVISING TEACHER

Of all the relationships in operation during student teaching, perhaps none is more important than that existing between the intern and the supervising teacher.[1a] The intern and master teacher[1b] must work and plan together on a daily basis. Together they decide what should be taught, when it should be taught, how it should be taught, and which materials should be used when teaching it. They confer about other critical matters such as how to motivate individual students as well as entire classes, how to best assist slow and bright learners, how to handle disciplinary problems, and how to counsel concerned parents.

1. BE AWARE THAT THE SUPERVISING TEACHER MAY BE SUPERIOR, MEDIOCRE, OR INFERIOR.

Because the supporting role of the supervising teacher is vital to the success of the student teacher, it should be expected that supervising teachers would be chosen with the greatest of care, that they would be chosen for their fresh instruction, their dedication to the pursuit of learning, and their love for children and youth. Too often, however, this is not the case. Frequently, the college director of student teaching assigns the intern to a local school system, and an administrative officer in the school system assigns him to any teacher who is willing to accept the responsibility of directing an intern throughout student teaching. Occasionally an intern will be assigned to a teacher who has not consented to accept the responsibility of supervising a student teacher. Such a haphazard method of choosing a supervising teacher is nothing short of a disgrace to the teaching profession. Be that as it may, before entering student teaching, the intern should realize that his supervising teacher may be superior, mediocre, or inferior. Fortunately, however, most supervising teachers are competent, dedicated, and highly professional.

Relating to the superior supervising teacher is generally simple and pleasurable, for this type of teacher (being enthusiastic, scholarly, innovative, sensitive to the needs of others, and cooperative) does all he can to enhance the instruction of the intern by lending full support to the instructional programs developed jointly by the two.

On the other hand, student teaching under a mediocre or poor supervising teacher may not be so enjoyable nor so easy. The poor teacher (frequently apathetic, unimaginative, rigid, and intellectually stagnant) is likely to be unreceptive to fresh instructional ideas and view with a degree of jealousy and envy an inventive, vigorous intern whose teaching may threaten to overshadow the insipid instruction of the supervising teacher. However, as early as possible the intern should assess the type of supervising teacher he has and be pragmatic when deciding how to relate to him, for the intern should realize that a harmonious partnership, forced or natural, is highly desirable and perhaps vital to the ultimate success of the student teacher; without the support and cooperation of the supervising teacher, the student teacher may find instructional and management problems mushrooming out of control. Observing a break between the intern and the supervising teacher, the students may lose respect for the intern, virtually ignoring him and seeking instruction and direction from the supervising teacher. In such an instance, a disgruntled supervising teacher could intensify the seriousness of the situation by encouraging such insulting student behavior.

Conversely, a cooperative, supportive supervising teacher would make clear to the students from the beginning that the student teacher is in charge of instruction and management in the classroom. If students should attempt to

46

circumvent the intern and seek direction from the supervising teacher, the alert supervising teacher would immediately remind the students that their teacher is the intern and that they should seek direction from him.

Therefore, whether the supervising teacher be professionally poor, mediocre, or superior, the intern should make every effort to see that the working relationship existing between himself and his supervising teacher is as smooth and harmonious as possible.

Another challenge facing the intern is that of operating within the framework of a classroom atmosphere already developed by the supervising teacher. Some supervising teachers create a highly formal atmosphere by being rigid, distant, excessively demanding, impersonal, and egoistic. Others set an atmosphere of near bedlam by having no organized instructional program and allowing excessive talking, shouting, and walking about in the classroom.

On the other hand, the model supervising teacher, realizing the important relationship of a proper classroom atmosphere to learning, attempts to be understanding, kind, patient, friendly, and creative in the development and use of instructional methods. The atmosphere he generates is conducive to comfort and relaxation. Although there are few classroom regulations, these are enforced with firmness, fairness, courtesy, and good judgment. Fortunate, indeed, is the intern who is privileged to enter a classroom where the supervising teacher has developed a positive classroom atmosphere which assists in the maximizing of learning.

Be Cautious When Attempting To Adjust The Classroom Atmosphere.

Be that as it may, the student teacher must be aware of the atmosphere set by the supervising teacher. Although the intern can do little or nothing to bring about major changes in a poor teaching atmosphere, with great care and caution, he may be able to make minor adjustments which could improve a classroom atmosphere that does not lend itself to a maximizing of learning. For instance, if the supervising teacher has allowed several students to answer a question at the same time and the result is that no one of them can be heard, with the greatest discretion, the intern may explain to the class that he wants every speaker to be heard, but he cannot understand any one of them when several respond at the same time. Therefore, the intern politely asks the students to raise their hands and be recognized before they share their views with the class. Or the supervising teacher may allow the students to sit where they wish from day to day. The intern, desiring to use a seating chart to facilitate his learning of students' names and to save time when taking roll, may ask each student to choose a seat and sit in that seat each day. Again, it is likely that both the students and the supervising teacher will give full co-operation.

Reduce Unnecessary Noise To a Tolerable Level.

There are some established classroom practices which the student teacher may be able to modify slightly, only. If, for example, the supervising teacher has allowed an <u>excessive</u> amount of unnecessary talking, the intern will find it nearly impossible to reduce this chatter to a level most conducive to learning. If the intern should go too far in his attempt to reduce the patter, the supervising teacher is not likely to cooperate nor are the students, who enjoy the chattering and realize that the supervising teacher is not likely to lend support to an "upstart" intern who is coming into the classroom and attempting to make radical changes in classroom policy and atmosphere. Consequently, in a situation such as this, normally the best an intern can hope for is to reduce unnecessary talking to what he considers a tolerable level.

2. *SEEK ASSISTANCE FROM THE SUPERVISING TEACHER*

Some supervising teachers prefer a "hands off" policy. They feel that during class they should be seen by the intern infrequently and that the intern should have full responsibility for such matters as developing teaching units,

48

preparing lesson plans, and evaluating the students' work. This type of supervising teacher usually believes that his primary responsibility is to be aware, generally, of the teaching program so that if an instructional or other emergency should arise, he could be available and prepared to step in and offer necessary assistance. Just as some swimmers believe that the best way to teach a non-swimmer to swim is to throw him into the water and force him to work out his own "salvation," so some supervising teachers think that the best way to help an intern learn to teach is to throw him into the classroom and force him to work out his own "pedagogical salvation."

Prepare To Adjust To The "Mother Hen" Supervising Teacher.

Other supervising teachers, the "mother hen" type, take a view opposite that of the "hands-off" supervising teacher. The "mother hen" supervisor is just as over-supportive as the "hands-off" type is under-supportive. The over-supportive teacher, fearful that the intern may do something "wrong" or not be able to "handle the situation," makes many decisions independently; these may range from organizational matters to curricular and instructional concerns. It is not unusual for this type of supervising teacher to dictate how the desks will be positioned, how many students may be out of the classroom at the same time, and how much of the windows will be covered by the shades. He may also tell the intern exactly what the students will study and the sequence in which they will study it, leaving only a few minor options for the student teacher to choose among.

Fortunately most supervising teachers are neither the "hands-off" type nor the "mother hen" type; rather, they understand that their primary role is to be that of a guide, evaluator, counselor, and friend.

Prepare To Adjust To The "Typical" Supervising Teacher.

The supervising teacher may be trusted first as an instructional guide because of his extensive professional preparation and abundance of experience in teaching. When planning the instructional program for the period of student teaching, the intern should seek direction from the master teacher in the developing of teaching techniques, instructional objectives, units of study, daily lesson plans, and in the construction and selection of instructional materials. The master teacher also stands ready to serve as a consultant should the intern need assistance in understanding certain areas of content. When going to the master teacher for assistance with problems relating to comprehension of subject matter, the intern should not be embarrassed, for the supervising teacher realizes that no intern can possibly master all areas of any discipline and also knows that the intern who seeks assistance can be helped because he recognizes his need, for recognition of one's need is the first step to the ultimate solving of any professional problem, be it instructional or otherwise.

Although classroom management is discussed in detail in Chapter Ten, it should be emphasized here that the master teacher is prepared to assist by giving suggestions that will help insure the smooth operation of learning activities in the classroom.

The significant point is that the intern should feel free to seek assistance from his master teacher, who is professionally prepared and usually eager to advise in matters of instruction, classroom management, and subject-matter content.

Seek Professional Evaluation.

Not only should the student teacher seek guidance in these areas, he should also realize that being a novice, he needs to have his teaching evaluated by an experienced professional. At the end of each teaching day, it is advisable for the intern to go to the master teacher and request an evaluation of the day's performance. The intern should seek and expect an objective evaluation, which identifies the intern's teaching strengths as well as areas that need improving. Of course, the student teacher is pleased to hear words of commendation, but he should be just as pleased to hear words of correction, for such suggestions are the stuff that promotes personal and professional growth. In addition to giving daily verbal evaluations, some master teachers also give daily, or periodic, written evaluations, a copy going to the master's files and another to the student teacher for study and filing.

At the end of each day, or whenever the master teacher thinks an evaluation is advisable, the two should sit down together for at least a half hour and discuss in detail the written evaluation. During each conference, most attention should focus on the instructional, subject matter, and disciplinary (human relations) problems that actually developed in the student teacher's classroom. The intern should feel free to ask questions of the supervising teacher and seek his advice concerning all types of classroom and related problems.

View Your Master Teacher As A Friend.

As well as being a professional counselor, many, perhaps most, master teachers want their student teachers to view them as friends, who are pleased to give of their personal time and experience for guidance in a host of non-professional problems that can range from finance to transportation. Look upon your master teacher as a personal friend as well as a professional counselor.

3. BE RESPONSIBLE TO SUPERIORS

Just as the supervising teacher has a responsibility to serve the intern, so the intern has a responsibility to the supervising teacher. The intern must not forget that he is a guest of the school system, the school, and, finally, the master teacher. To demonstrate his appreciation for the opportunity to gain first-hand teaching experience, the intern should always cooperate with and show respect for school officials and the master teacher, even though, at times, he may feel that the school's rules or the master teacher's suggestions are inadvisable or even foolish.

Not only will the intern's full cooperation with school officials and the master teacher make for a harmonious relationship, but it will also help create a positive, warm, congenial classroom atmosphere that will go far in promoting a maximum level of learning.

[1a,b]Throughout this book the terms "supervising teacher" and "master teacher" are used interchangeably.

CHAPTER 8

Who is the college student teaching counselor and what are his functions? Answers to these two fundamental questions are offered in this chapter.

1. KNOW THE FUNCTION OF THE STUDENT TEACHING COUNSELOR

The college or university counselor is a professional educator employed by the teacher training institution at which the intern is enrolled when he is doing his student teaching. Some teacher training institutions provide two counselors for their secondary student teachers. One counselor, often called the "supervisor," is a member of the education department, and the other counselor, frequently referred to as the "consultant," is a member of a department representing a given discipline such as history, English, physical education, or mathematics.

Know The Role Of The Supervisor.

When the teacher training institution provides both a supervisor and a consultant, the primary function of the supervisor is to advise the student teacher in general educational matters. Such advice may have to do with the developing of instructional goals, units of study, lesson plans, teaching techniques, and classroom management procedures.

Know The Role Of The Consultant.

Although the consultant will concern himself with any or all of these areas also, his basic responsibility is to give counsel in the academic discipline which he represents. The consultant is prepared to assist in solving problems having to do with the selecting, the understanding, the sequencing, and the presenting of content as well as the developing and procuring of instructional materials. The consultant also assists with problems growing out of the evaluating of student performance.

Teacher training institutions that do not provide both a college consultant and a college supervisor will, nonetheless, provide a college supervisor who will give counsel in general educational affairs as well as in matters having to do with academic content. Fortunate, indeed, is the student teacher whose college provides both a general education supervisor and a content consultant, for the generalist and the specialist can cooperate to give expert counsel to the student teacher.

2. *CONSIDER THE STUDENT TEACHING COUNSELOR A FRIEND*

The intern should not only view his student teaching counselor as an educational expert, but he should consider the counselor a friend as well. The student teacher should understand that this friendship is based primarily on two factors. First, many, perhaps most, counselors want to be friendly and helpful because they, recalling their frustrations as student teachers and how much they appreciated their counselor's assistance, wish to make the student teaching experience as pleasant and rewarding as possible. Second, it is natural for a friendship to blossom between the counselor and intern since they are both seeking the same goal, success for the student. To a great extent, when the student teacher succeeds, the college's teacher training program and the college student teaching counselor succeed, but when the student teacher fails, so do the college and the counselor. Therefore, the intern may confidently look to the college counselor as a mentor and a friend.

3. *SEEK GUIDANCE EARLY*

However, the student teacher should not wait until he begins student teaching to draw upon the advice of the college counselor. Early in the semester preceding student teaching, the student should set up at least one conference with the college counselor if the counselor has not been the student's methods professor. If the student is being taught methods by the one who is to counsel him during student teaching, one or more conferences should take place automatically within the framework of the class since one major objective of many methods classes is to help prepare the student for the student teaching experience. On the other hand, if the student's methods teacher will not be his student teaching counselor, a conference preceding student teaching is definitely advantageous. At this conference the student should feel free to raise any questions that may concern him about any aspect of student teaching or related matters. The student will normally find the counselor receptive, informed, and willing to help solve any problems and allay any fears that may detract from a successful student teaching experience.

Anticipate Early Group Guidance.

Also, at the beginning of the semester, the college counselor normally has a group meeting with all the students who will intern during that semester. At this meeting, the counselor explains that his visits to the intern's classes will be for supervisory purposes, not "snoopervisory" purposes. He discusses such matters as the number of visits he will make to the intern's classroom, when he will make these, what he will look for, and how his visits will be designed to strengthen the teaching of the intern.

4. DEVELOP A SMOOTH WORKING RELATIONSHIP WITH THE COUNSELOR

Becoming acquainted with the college counselor and seeking his advice before student teaching begins is clearly advisable. It is absolutely essential, however, that the student teacher do all within his power to develop a smooth working relationship during the internship with the college counselor, for it is the counselor who will offer the latest professional advice, give a final grade for student teaching, and write an evaluation that will become part of the student teacher's permanent college records. These records will, of course, follow the student throughout his professional career and be carefully studied by most, perhaps all, prospective employers.

A few days after the intern leaves the college campus, settles into his apartment, and begins working with the master teacher, the college counselor may be expected to visit the classroom and confer jointly or individually with both the master teacher and the intern. The purposes of this conference are: (1) to give the master teacher opportunity to share his initial impressions and concerns with the intern and the counselor, (2) to give the intern opportunity to ask questions of and receive feedback from both the master teacher and the counselor, and (3) to give the college counselor an early opportunity to meet the master teacher and assess such matters as: how harmoniously the intern and master teacher are working together, how well the intern and students are re- lating, and how well the intern is adjusting to the general teaching situation.

5. *LOOK FORWARD TO THE COUNSELOR'S VISITS*

After this initial conference, the intern may expect the college counselor to visit the classroom from one to several times each week. When the counselor visits the classroom, he may or may not give the intern advance notice; however, early in the student teaching experience, it is likely that he will indicate in advance the day, and possibly the period, when he will be arriving. The coun- selor is likely to arrive at the classroom a few minutes before class is to be- gin so that he will not disturb the lesson once it has begun. When he enters the classroom, the intern should introduce him to the master teacher and to the students. The student teacher should provide the counselor an empty desk or table at the back of the classroom; from this position his presence is least likely to detract from the lesson. At the same time, this position allows him to have a full view of all class members as well as any activities taking place during the lesson.

After the counselor is seated, the intern should offer him a copy of all lesson plans, including those for the current lesson as well as those leading up to the current lesson. If the student teacher is having the students use a textbook or written handouts during the lesson, he should see to it that the college counselor has a copy of each.

As the student teacher proceeds with the lesson, the college counselor may be expected to take notes on the activities of the period.

Anticipate A Post-Lesson Conference

After the lesson and while the master teacher instructs the class during the next period, it is normal for the college counselor and the intern to go into a conference. During the conference the college counselor gives the student teacher opportunity to assess his current pedagogic performance and measure the value of the student teaching experience to this point. The college counselor, himself, will broach such topics as: (1) The clarity and specificity of the intern's instructional objectives, (2) The relationship of the instructional objectives to the learning needs of the students, (3) The adequacy of the intern's lesson plans,[2] (4) The adequacy of preparation by the intern for the lesson, (5) The methods used to spark student participation, (6) The amount of student participation generated, (7) The levels of questions[3] asked by the student teacher, (8) The ability of the intern to interact freely with the class during discussion, (9) The skill of the student teacher in selecting instructional materials in keeping with the instructional goals and students' needs and aptitude, (10) The ability of the intern to answer thoroughly and clearly questions put to him by the students, (11) The capacity of the student teacher to interest students in the lesson, (12) The teaching style of the intern, (13) The flair of the intern for managing a class that is orderly, yet not stiff and formal, (14) The ability of the intern to act calmly and prudently when unexpected emergencies arise within the classroom, and (15) The skill of the student teacher in working harmoniously with the supervising teacher and other school personnel.

During the conference, the college counselor may also be expected to emphasize the major strengths of the lesson. In addition, he will note areas of the lesson that are weak and offer recommendations which will make for improvement in these areas. After the oral evaluation of the intern's instructional performance for the period, the college counselor should then give the student teacher a written copy of the evaluation, which served as a basis for his comments during the conference. At the earliest possible time, the intern should study carefully and in detail this written evaluation, being cognizant of the commendations as well as the suggestions that would improve the instruction. The student teacher should be aware that during the college counselor's next visit, he will expect the intern to show improvement in his teaching by implementing suggestions made by the counselor during his previous visit.

Expect The College Counselor To Confer With The Supervising Teacher.

As well as meeting frequently with the intern, the college counselor will also meet periodically with the supervising teacher so that they may evaluate jointly the intern's performance. If the two feel that the student teacher is experiencing serious problems in one or more areas, they will, no doubt, schedule a conference with the intern so that all three may discuss the matter face-to-face. In such a conference, not only will problems be identified, but corrective recommendations will also be offered to the student teacher.

Expect Three-Way Conferences.

The intern should not assume, however, that if he should be asked to meet jointly with both the college counselor and the master teacher that they have identified and wish to discuss a serious pedagogic problem. Some counselors and master teachers meet routinely in a three-way conference with the student teacher for the purpose of: exchanging views so as to solve minor instructional problems before they become major, strengthening the professional relationship among the three, and unifying their approach to the broad pedagogical challenges facing the student teacher.

6. *TAKE ADVANTAGE OF THE COUNSELOR'S ASSISTANCE*

Another service offered by the college counselor is providing some instructional materials for the intern. Because of budgetary limitations few, if any, college counselors are able to provide unlimited instructional materials; however, they may be expected to make available copies of such items as instructional games, audio-visual sources, appropriate articles from professional journals, and pertinent bibliographies. If the intern needs certain instructional materials which are not available from the local school system in which he is teaching, he should feel free to ask his college counselor for information that would guide him to the needed materials.

7. *EXPECT THE COUNSELOR TO EVALUATE TEACHING SKILL*

The college counselor's responsibilities do not cease when the intern finishes his student teaching. The counselor and master teacher must then write evaluations of the student teacher's performance. A copy of these evaluations may be expected to go to the student teacher and, in some instances, to the college director of placement, who puts the evaluations in the student teacher's credentials' file for the benefit of prospective employers and graduate schools to which the intern may apply for admission.

As a post student teaching service, some colleges are now providing a follow-up program, which continues offering the former intern guidance by the college counselor during the first year of teaching.

In summary, the student teacher should view the college student teaching counselor as a friendly and professional educator who is dedicated to serving the student teacher and doing all within his power to make sure that the student teacher's internship is indeed rewarding, enjoyable, and, in the end, a sufficient introduction to full-time classroom instruction.

[1] In this book "counselor" refers to both the "college supervisor" and the "college consultant", each of whom is discussed in this chapter.

[2] See Glossary "C" for model lesson plan.

[3] Higher levels of questions require the student answering the questions to employ comprehension, analysis, synthesis, evaluation, or substantiated opinion. Lower level questions require identification, recall, or unsubstantiated opinion. For a detailed discussion of levels of questions, see the doctoral dissertation "The Types of Oral Questions Asked by Student Teachers of Literature at the Eight, Ninth, and Tenth Grade Levels" by the author of this book. This dissertation is available on microfilm from University Microfilms, Ann Arbor, Michigan.

CHAPTER 9

RELATING TO THE STUDENTS AND PARENTS

The relationship between the intern and the students and their parents is crucial because how the students and parents perceive the intern will go far in determining the amount of learning that will take place in the classroom.

1. BUILD A POSITIVE STUDENT ATTITUDE

If the students feel that the intern is distant, apathetic, arrogant, or unprepared for class, they will not respect him as a person or a professional. Consequently, a psychological, emotional, or cognitive barrier is likely to develop and short-circuit learning. On the other hand, if the students believe the student teacher to be friendly, but not chummy; enthusiastic, but not gushing; kind but not spineless; learned but not bookish; and wise, but not crafty, they are likely to love and respect him. Such a positive student attitude will, of course, go far in maximizing learning.

Avoid Activities Which Detract From Teaching.

There are still other ways to promote a positive student attitude toward the intern and learning. The student teacher should recognize that his first duty is to instruct the students. Any personal, social, or peripheral professional activities which substantially interfere with this responsibility should be curtailed as soon as proper arrangements allow such to be done.

Be Fair, Friendly, And Helpful.

Other ways for the intern to build a strong positive relationship between himself and his students are: (1) to be fair and objective when evaluating the students' work (give the student the benefit of any doubt), (2) to be patient with all students, even those who are most trying, (3) to be respectful and courteous (remember, students are first of all people who are worthy of esteem), (4) to avoid playing favorites even though the student teacher's feelings may prompt him to do otherwise, (5) to show a good sense of humor, (6) and to be of personal service to any student in need of the student teacher's assistance.

2. *LEARN THE BROAD TYPES OF STUDENTS EARLY*

The student teacher's skill in relating successfully to many classes of students is tested daily. The broad types of students may be divided into at least nine categories.

Recognize The Intelligent, Cooperative Student.

First, there is the highly intelligent student who is serious, studious, dependable, self-directing, and cooperative. Relating to this type of student usually presents no problems. The student teacher needs, mostly, to give direction to the student's work and be prepared to guide him to learning resources which he may be expected to avidly exhaust.

Recognize The Intelligent, Uncooperative Student.

The second kind of student is also highly intelligent, but likely to be uncooperative or even cantankerous. Since such a student is frequently quarrelsome because he is underchallenged and, therefore, bored, the student teacher should give him more challenging work and offer sincere praise when an assignment is well done. This approach should not only make learning enjoyable for the student but should also make him feel a sense of accomplishment that is likely to make for a more positive attitude toward both learning and the student teacher.

Recognize The Average, Well Motivated Student.

A third class of student is of average intelligence, well motivated, and studious. Like the cooperative student of high intelligence, this third type of student needs careful guidance, but, in addition, he needs frequent personal assistance because he often meets learning problems which he alone cannot solve.

Recognize The Average, Apathetic Student.

The fourth type of student is also of average intelligence, but instead of finding learning a joy, he is apathetic and indifferent. Therefore, the major challenge facing the student teacher in this instance is one of generating interest. In order to help the student shake off his lethargy, the intern needs to employ individualized instruction. This may be done by discovering the interests of the student and, as far as possible, relating the assignments to the student's interests. Such an approach, drawing upon motivation that is already existent, should go far in making learning appealing and enjoyable. When learning becomes fun for the student, the intern can be certain that the student's apathy has been broken and that he is well on his way to working to capacity.

Recognize The Below Average, Industrious Student.

A fifth kind of student is one who is below average in intelligence but who, valuing learning and wanting to please his parents and teachers, applies himself fully. In order to be of most help to this type of student, the intern should praise the student for his enthusiasm, initiative, and progress and give him as much personal assistance as time will allow.

Recognize The Below Average, Unmotivated Student.

The sixth class of student, being of below average intelligence and lacking motivation, is likely to be troublesome since he has seldom tasted the sweetness of success in his school work. In this case the intern will need to motivate the student. This may be done by (1) giving him work that is on his level (work that he is capable of doing) and (2) guiding him into assignments that will draw heavily upon interests he already has. Such an approach may be expected to show this type of student the pleasure of learning and help him make a normal adjustment to the classroom situation.

Recognize The Retarded Student.

A seventh type of student, found infrequently in the typical classroom, is the one of extremely limited intelligence, the retarded pupil. Because the student teacher has probably had little or no training in the instruction of such persons, because of inadequate facilities and instructional materials, and because of a lack of time, the student teacher, suspecting intellectual retardation, should not attempt to handle such a problem alone but should suggest to the supervising teacher, school nurse, or administration that the pupil be referred to the school psychiatrist, who, in turn, may place the student in a special education program. If the school system in which the intern is student teaching has no psychiatrist or special education program, except for rare exceptions, the intern must resign himself to the role of "baby sitting" for this particular type of pupil. The student teacher should not be expected to meet such overwhelming demands which the school board and other administrative officers have not seem fit to address.

Recognize The Hyper-Active Student.

An eighth type of student found frequently at the elementary and junior high school levels, especially, is the hyper-active pupil. This class of student is made up of persons representing a wide spectrum of intellectual levels from the dull to the bright. The student teacher should provide such a student as many opportunities as possible to work off his excess energy; however, the intern should be aware that this kind of problem may very well have physical or emotional roots. Consequently, when the intern observes a given student being chronically hyper-active, he should alert the supervising teacher or school nurse, who may, in turn, arrange for the student to see a physician and/or psychiatrist.

Recognize The Withdrawing Student.

The intern will discover a ninth kind of student to be retiring and withdrawn. This type of student, also representing all intellectual levels, is likely to be moody, silent, and gloomy. Again, if the student teacher is unable to break this chronic dejection by conferences and a sincere attempt at consumating a friendship, the intern should call the problem to the attention of the master teacher or school nurse so that professional help may be arranged if such is considered advisable.

Although these nine categories of student types are not intended to be exhaustive and even though there will be overlapping of types, they will serve to alert the student teacher to the fact that students' abilities and personalities are vastly different. Recognizing this, the intern can prepare to individualize instruction as much as possible as well as look for and adjust to the varied mixes of personalities and intellectual levels found among students at the elementary, junior high, and senior high school levels.[1]

2. BUILD POSITIVE PARENTAL RELATIONS

Not only should the student teacher attempt to relate positively to his students, but he should also put forth every effort to create an amiable relationship with the parents or guardians of his students. The intern should view the parents as his partners in the teaching-learning process. Although there are exceptions, generally, parents are greatly concerned about their children's progress in school.

Meet The Parents.

The intern should, of course, seize upon every opportunity to meet his students' parents. By attending P.T.A. meetings and as many other school functions as possible and by visiting selected students' homes, the student teacher will have opportunity to become personally acquainted with many parents.

Keep Parents Informed.

Recognizing the parental interest in the pupil's welfare, the intern should give early and serious consideration to contacting the parents of any student experiencing learning, social, or emotional problems. Parents can frequently provide information and guidance that will assist the intern in solving motivational, instructional, social, or disciplinary problems. For instance, during the first year of teaching, the author was at his wits end to know how to get the cooperation and respect of a talented, intelligent girl in a high school class. After a number of attempts at solving the problem alone, he decided to visit the student's home and reveal to the parents the problems he was encountering. After finding the mother home and explaining to her the trouble her daughter was generating, he was pleased when the mother assured him that she knew nothing of such unruly conduct by her daughter and that she and her husband would speak with the girl that very night. Apparently the parents lived up to the mother's promise, for from the next class period until the end of the school year, the once troublesome student was polite, respectful, and cooperative. Needless to say, the girl's grades improved and the entire class benefitted when the tension that once pervaded the classroom was replaced by an atmosphere of cooperation and harmony.

Schedule Parent-Teacher Conferences.

The student teacher should also make himself available for parent-teacher conferences. If these conferences are scheduled in the evening and if parents are invited to make appointments in advance, the intern is likely to generate parental interest and obtain limited, but sufficient, participation. In these conferences, the student teacher should objectively report the students' strengths and needs and invite questions from the parents. If the intern thinks that parental cooperation would help solve a particular learning or disciplinary problem, he should feel free to discuss the problem with the parents, recommend a solution, and request the cooperation of the parents in helping solve the problem.

Be Courteous, Objective, Firm And Fair.

Whenever the intern finds himself facing disgruntled, bad-tempered, irate parents, he should determine that he will always: (1) be polite and courteous, (2) attempt to discover why the parents are perturbed, (3) provide a clear, reasonable explanation for any intern-inniated action under discussion, (4) correct any inadvertent error, (5) hold firm to the earlier position if no error or mistake in judgement is involved, and (6) conclude the discussion by being reasonable and firm.

Be Professional; Practice Confidentiality.

In any conference the student teacher should discuss the student's conduct, rate of progress, and grades with the concerned student's parents only. Parents who bring up the issue of conduct or grades of pupils who are not their children, should be reminded that information about other parents' children is strictly confidential. Therefore, the student teacher should never allow certain parents to draw him into a position where he is comparing their children's work or conduct with the work or conduct of other parents' children.

The intern should ever remember that a poor relationship between himself and the students and their parents detracts from the teaching-learning process, but a strong, positive relationship promotes good will and advances learning.

FOOTNOTES--CHAPTER IX

[1]Herbert J. Klausmeier, <u>Teaching In The Secondary School</u> (New York: Harper and Brothers, 1958), pp. 401-407.

CHAPTER 10

CLASSROOM MANAGEMENT

The intern becomes the classroom <u>manager</u> as soon as the class is given over to him by the master teacher. As classroom manager, the student teacher becomes responsible for the direction and regulation of all activities in the classroom. This means that the intern must plan, organize, and direct both instructional and non-instructional affairs, for without adequate leadership the atmosphere of any classroom may be expected to regress into chaos.

1. *SET A POSITIVE ATMOSPHERE*

For maximum learning to take place, the classroom atmosphere should be relaxed, comfortable, warm, free of tension, and untroubled. Perhaps the best way for the intern to set such an atmosphere is for him (1) to radiate an air of confidence and (2) to organize carefully classroom activities.

Be Confident.

In order for the student teacher to enter his classroom emitting confidence, he must have a positive self image. That is, he, himself, must believe that his training and personal qualities are such that he will be able, with the professional assistance provided by the local school system and the college, to instruct and manage his classes successfully. Such confidence need not be groundless, for the student teacher should recall that he has had extensive training in both teaching methods and subject matter content; in addition, he has had some, perhaps much, experience observing how professional, experienced teachers conduct routine and instructional matters as well as deal with various types of disciplinary problems.

Keep Accurate Attendance Records.

A well organized classroom also facilitates learning because it allows routine matters to be handled efficiently and with a minimum of confusion. Take, for example, the matter of keeping an accurate record of attendance. If the student teacher simply looks over the class and from memory tries to spot absentees, he is likely to overlook a missing student. However, if he uses a seating chart when checking attendance, the record will be accurate and taken with dispatch.[1]

Keep Accurate Records Of Money.

Likewise, frequently the student teacher will be required to collect money from students for such items as books, magazines, or tickets. A lack of organization in such an instance often causes a great deal of confusion and results in the loss of much valuable time and energy that should be given to instruction. For instance, money may be collected efficiently by furnishing each student with an envelope on which he writes his name and the date and in which he puts his money. After these things have been done, the student teacher, or a responsible student, then walks up and down the aisles collecting the envelopes. While doing this, he checks to see that the money is enclosed and makes certain that the necessary information is on each envelope. This procedure--orderly, accurate, and quick--allows the student teacher to record the necessary information at a later, more convenient time if he so chooses.

Have Students Sit Quietly During Announcements.

Announcement time can also spark turbulence and confusion. Every school has its own time for announcements and its own method of giving announcements. Some schools set aside time each day to have announcements read early each morning or near the close of the school day over the public address system. Other schools have their announcements read in each classroom by the teacher or student. No matter when or how announcements are handled, the intern should insist that the students sit quietly during announcement time, for when some students are milling about, sharpening pencils, and talking, neither they nor those sitting quietly listening are likely to hear the information being given in the announcements.

2. *PLAN SMALL GROUP ACTIVITIES*

Because learning psychologists have discovered that actively involving the students in learning activities aids them in mastering that which is being taught, the student teacher will want to consider devoting a substantial part of class time to involving the students in various kinds of small group activities. Whether these activities consist of panel discussions, study groups, the organizing of musical programs, the writing and producing of plays, or preparing reports, analyses, and evaluations, the intern should develop in writing his instructional goals for each group, a time-frame for the achieving of the goals, a list of community persons who may be drawn upon as resources, and a plan for evaluating whether or not the instructional goals were reached.

Carefully Choose And Place Students.

Another important part of managing small group activities is the choosing and placing of students. Students who can work well together should be mixed into the small group as should brighter and slower students. The usual enthusiasm of the brighter students tends to favorably influence the usual apathy of many slower students, and the leadership and resourcefulness of the more intelligent ones give the work of the entire group purpose, motivation, and direction. Failure to plan carefully and well in advance can lead to managerial disaster for the intern dividing his students for group work.

Give Assistance.

After the groups are formed, organized, and functioning, the student teacher should "float" about the room, keeping in touch with the needs and progress of each group and offering to help solve problems that the students, themselves, are unable to resolve. For instance, members of one group preparing a panel discussion based on questions growing out of their reading, may disagree among themselves on the "correct" answer to a given question. Members of another group making costumes for a Thanksgiving play may want design suggestions. A third group preparing choral readings of Hebrew poetry may want to know the definition of the term "selah,"[2] which frequently appears in the Psalms. In such instances, the intern may suggest solutions, himself, or direct students to sources which would assist them in solving their own problems.

Plan Evaluation Procedures.

Finally, the intern needs to evaluate the work produced by each group to determine if the instructional goals have been achieved. These goals will, themselves, guide the student teacher in determining the method of evaluation. If, for instance, the intern is evaluating a panel discussion, the quality of the individual's answers is the primary point of focus; if he is evaluating student-made costumes, the authenticity of their design and aesthetic matters are of greatest interest. Unless there is good reason for doing otherwise, the student teacher should give each member of a small group a grade based on the quality and amount of work displayed by that student. Grading in this manner demands that the intern be aware of the contribution of each member to the group's activities.

The student teacher who pre-plans and carefully organizes such activities will discover the secret to efficiently managing small study groups.

3. AVOID EXTREMES IN CLASSROOM MANAGEMENT

Although the intern spends much time directing small groups, even more of his time is likely to be spent managing the entire class. To make for a smoothly operating class, the student teacher should avoid both extreme authoritarianism and extreme libertarianism.

Don't Be The Army Sergeant.

The student teacher who is inclined to command his students as would an army sergeant his recruits, is likely to evoke resentment from those, especially, who tend to be creative and independent in their thinking. The intern should make the students feel that all serious viewpoints are welcome and may be presented to and examined by the class. The intern, not expecting that other's ideas will always agree with his, should not become testy or sulky when students politely and respectfully pose a point of view out of harmony with his own.

Handle Moot Topics Fairly.

On the other hand, the student teacher who allows moot viewpoints to be discussed freely should also require that issues be handled tastefully, fairly, and orderly.

4. *GIVE ATTENTION TO THE PHYSICAL ENVIRONMENT*

Management of one's students also includes providing a cheerfully decorated classroom. Such a classroom assists in promoting a positive student attitude toward the school, the subject, the intern, and learning itself. It is no secret, of course, that dark, dull rooms make for gloominess and depression. On the other hand, colorful bulletin boards, pictures, flower arrangements, and book jackets can help brighten any classroom.

Adjust Blinds And Windows.

Blinds should be adjusted so as to admit an appropriate amount of light, and the temperature should be comfortable in both cold and hot weather. When building design permits, windows should be adjusted to allow for an abundance of fresh air.

5. *SEEK RESPECT*

Adding to the managerial talents of the intern is his ability to have personal rapport with his students. Such a harmonious relationship can be strengthened by the intern: (1) who cultivates a clear, projecting voice; (2) who avoids avant-garde dress but displays good taste and neatness; (3) who is able to laugh at himself; (4) who avoids annoying mannerisms; and (5) who is content to be himself, yet by frequent self evaluation, always attempting to improve himself personally and professionally.

6. *PREPARE FOR MINOR DISCIPLINARY CHALLENGES*

Frequently the intern will need to address himself to disciplinary problems, especially "minor" disciplinary problems, which may be defined as those human relations problems that normally may be solved by the student teacher, himself, within the classroom.

Prevent Disciplinary Problems.

When facing any disciplinary problem, the intern should first attempt to find and correct the <u>cause</u> of the undesirable behavior. Just as <u>prevention</u> is the best cure in medicine, so is prevention the best "cure" for disciplinary problems in the classroom. As is discussed in the next chapter, using fresh instructional methods and selecting appropriate study materials are the best ways to prevent unacceptable behavior.

Assess The Degree Of Instructional Appeal.

Among the most frequently occurring minor disciplinary problems are excessive student noise, excessive student movement about the classroom, and unacceptable language. Although ignoring isolated instances or minor infringements upon human relations norms is sometimes advisable, there are times when such problems must be dealt with. However, before contemplating punitive action, <u>always</u> assess the degree of instructional appeal being made to the problem student. If the learning activity is dull, over-challenging or under-challenging, the intern may need to change the pace of the learning activity, shift to another activity, or move this student to a level of subject matter in keeping with realistic instructional goals and the ability and interests of the disinterested student. Never forget that a <u>busy</u>, <u>happy</u> <u>student</u> <u>is</u> <u>not</u> <u>a</u> <u>problem</u> <u>student</u>. A student <u>cannot</u> be happy if he feels he is wasting his time (being under-challenged) or if he feels he cannot cope with the material or learning activity at hand (being over-challenged).

Prepare To Deal With Excessive "Noise-makers."

Since excessive student noise can interrupt, or even halt, learning, the intern must deal firmly but fairly with those students responsible. If, for example, a student is rapping his desk with a ruler or patting his foot on the floor, a stern look from the intern or a courteous personal request for the student to stop the noise is usually successful. If the student is talking too much and a polite, personal request for him to stop is not effective, he may be moved to a location where he is surrounded by students who control their talking. Or, the intern may wish to stand by the student until he is drawn into the learning activity and forgets about his attempt to interrupt the class.

Prepare To Deal With Excessive "Walkers."

Excessive student movement about the classroom can also detract from learning. A few simple rules enforced consistently and fairly from the outset will go far in keeping this problem to a minimum. One student only should be allowed to go to the pencil sharpener at a time; one student only should be permitted to leave the room at a time; and except at specific times or unless special permission is given, one student only should be allowed to use the classroom library at a time.

Prepare To Deal With "Throwers."

From the beginning the student teacher should make it clear that nothing is to be thrown in the classroom and explain the reasons for this regulation. Thrown objects can, of course, cause serious physical harm to persons in the room and can also damage or destroy fragile objects such as light fixtures, vases, and window panes.

Prepare To Deal With "Swearers."

Because language is vital to the carrying on of human relationships and the teaching-learning process, language, of necessity, is indispensable in the classroom. Language, like other things that are of themselves good, may be misused. In the classroom certain language, of course, is appropriate, and certain language is inappropriate. From the very first class period, the intern should make it clear that name-calling, cursing, swearing, and all forms of abusive language are intolerable. If after ample guidance and warning a student continues to use unacceptable language in the classroom, the intern should give serious consideration to punishing the student; if the student does not respond to mild forms of punishment, the student teacher should then arrange to have the school counselor or psychologist and, if necessary, the parents, assistant principal, or the principal work with the student, attempting to find the cause of the misbehavior. As far as possible, however, these "minor" problems should be handled by the intern, himself.

7. PREPARE FOR MAJOR DISCIPLINARY CHALLENGES

Although most disciplinary problems are of a "minor" nature, at times the intern may expect to encounter "major" disciplinary problems. These types of problems may be defined as those human relations problems which normally cannot be solved by the student teacher, himself, within the structure of the classroom setting. Two examples of this type of problem are: (1) fighting between students and (2) a threat or attempt by a student to assault another student or the student teacher. Such aggressive behavior is a clear indication that the aggressor has deep-seated emotional problems which the student teacher is not trained to handle; therefore, students engaging in such threats or activities need the guidance of a professional trained in the handling of emotionally disturbed students. Every school should have such a person on its professional staff. In some schools the counselor is prepared professionally to work with aggressive students; in other schools the principal and assistant principal have such training. Be that as it may, before the intern takes over any class, he should acquaint himself with how to handle such referrals and to whom he should direct aggressive students. The intern can not expel a student; only the proper administrator, by authority granted him by the school board, can do this.

Be Familiar With The Appropriate Legal Codes.

Also, before the intern assumes responsibility for teaching any class, he should acquaint himself with the legal rights and responsibilities of teachers in the state where he will be teaching. Such information is usually available at no cost from the office of the county superintendent, the city superintendent, the state superintendent, the county attorney, the city attorney, or the attorney general.

Be Covered By Personal Liability Insurance.

The intern should be covered for personal liability while teaching. If the liability insurance of the system in which he is to teach does not cover student teachers, the intern should be sure that his college or university carries liability insurance that will cover him while he is student teaching. Although it is highly unlikely that a parent or student would carry a complaint to court, there is the possibility that such could be done. The intern covered by liability insurance is likely to be a more effective teacher since he doesn't have to worry about where he would get funds to defend himself should an action of his be challenged.

Maintain Self-Control.

An intern should never invite legal action by rash words or deeds which are likely to spring from anger. Therefore, the student teacher should always maintain self-control; if, on the other hand, the student teacher discovers that he is angry, he should wait until his anger has subsided before placing guilt or assigning punishment.

Follow These Practices.

The following suggestions should aid the student teacher in successfully managing his classroom:

1. Prevent disciplinary problems by having a planned, well prepared, fresh instructional program designed to meet the needs of <u>all</u> students.

2. Have few rules and enforce them with kindness, fairness, firmness, and consistency.

3. Use seating charts.

4. Make a conscious effort early to learn and use students' names.

5. Treat students as you wanted to be treated when you were an elementary or high school student.

6. Train students to be responsible for certain routine classroom responsibilities.

7. Avoid partiality.

8. Cultivate a pleasant voice with adequate volume.

9. Dress appropriately for the occasion.

10. Be friendly, but don't become too chummy with your students.

11. When in doubt, seek guidance from the supervising teacher or the college supervisor.

12. Return students' papers promptly.

13. Prepare <u>more</u> learning activities than you think you will need for any given period. (You don't want to run out of activities before the closing bell.)

14. Make a good impression from the very first day; be self-confident.

15. Have all instructional materials prepared in advance.

16. Open and close class on time.

17. Be aware of and use established referral procedures.

18. Frequently evaluate your managerial techniques, making adjustments where necessary.

19. Involve students in instructional and social activities.

20. Have a place for everything and keep each thing in its place.

21. Maintain a positive working relation with the supervising teacher.

Although the student teacher should work to have a well managed and organized classroom, he should avoid over-organization and regimentation, which can stifle student interest in learning and make the classroom a "jail" instead of a laboratory, a "prison" rather than a niche where students may, through searching, discover the joy of exploration as they sort out their talents, interests, and goals.

[1] For a discussion of seating charts, see Chapter VI, pp 40-43.

[2] See Glossary C, Definitions of Terms.

CHAPTER 11

MAJOR INSTRUCTIONAL MATTERS

Of all areas of teaching, perhaps none is so crucial for both the intern and student as the matter of instruction, for instruction is the very heart of the teaching-learning process. A student may be able to progress without a building, furnishings, and learning materials, but he can ill afford to do without the challenge, encouragement, correction, guidance, interest, and kindness of an instructor. Or, to put it in other terms, more learning may be expected to take place when a student is being taught by an intellectually stimulating teacher under an oak tree than by a disinterested, apathetic instructor teaching in the finest classroom with the most modern instructional materials.

1. MAKE LEARNING ACTIVE

The student teacher should also keep clearly in mind that learning is not something a teacher does to the student. Seldom, if ever, is learning a passive process only, requiring that the teacher "pour" knowledge from his "full receptacle" into the student's "empty receptacle." Learning is active. Learning is an intellectual or emotional experience (or a combination of the two) going on inside the learner, himself. Therefore, generally speaking, the most effective instruction actively involves the student in thinking and doing. The teacher cannot learn for the student; the student must learn for himself.

2. MOTIVATE THE STUDENT

In order for the student to learn, he, himself, must choose to learn, and his commitment to that choice may be called motivation. Since there are degrees of commitment, there are also degrees of motivation. Students who have almost no commitment to learning may be expected to be poorly motivated, while students strongly committed to learning are normally highly motivated. Although the decision to learn must be made by the student, himself, the intern can do some things that will strengthen a student's commitment to expanding his learning.

Become Familiar With Every Student.

Because every individual enjoys learning <u>something</u>, the intern should attempt to become familiar with every student. He should know both the student's learning needs and his interests and try to match these two by drawing upon those interests when leading the student toward the instructional goals set for that student. Remember, it is much easier to capitalize upon existing student interests than to generate new interests.

Be Enthusiastic.

There are other things which the student teacher can do to encourage motivation. First, interest and enthusiasm are catching. A student teacher who is interested in and enthusiastic about a topic will generate, in varying degrees, interest and enthusiasm in his students.

Choose Interesting Topics.

Second, the intern should attempt to choose study topics that are likely to be of interest to the age group being taught.

Allow Students To Choose Topics.

Third, frequently the student teacher should allow the students, themselves, to participate in choosing subject matter to be studied.

Use Community Resources.

Fourth, drawing upon experts in the community can often stimulate interest in study topics.

Use A-V Aids.

Finally, relating books, pictures, films, and other audio-visual aids to the topic being studied will assist in generating student interest.

Recognize Excellence.

The joy of learning is an adequate long-term, intrinsic reward that normally is preferred over external, short-term artificial stimuli such as grades, money, or food. However, quality work should always be appreciated and recognized privately or publicly, for all students wish to be and deserve to be recognized for excellent work.

Make Learning Fun.

Encourage a positive attitude toward learning. Remember, play is viewed as enjoyable, but work may be considered activity from which little or no joy is derived. As an intern do all within your power to make learning enjoyable; choose games which allow the student to compete with himself for progress toward and eventual mastery of the selected learning goal.

3. *CONSIDER WHAT TO TEACH*

Another major instructional concern of the intern is deciding what to teach. Since there is an overwhelming amount of fact, information, and opinion available in most areas of study, the intern must decide which of these to emphasize, give cursory attention, or ignore completely. Although deciding what to teach is a complex question, there are several fundamental guidelines which the student teacher should consider when addressing himself to this problem.

Consider The Goals Of The School System.

Initially, the intern should inform himself of the educational goals that the school system has set for the "typical" student at a given grade level. These goals are usually set forth in syllabi published and distributed by the school system. Frequently the educational goals presented in these syllabi are general in nature, allowing the student teacher a great deal of flexibility when deciding what to teach.

Emphasize The Basics And Practical.

While staying within the framework of the syllabi's goals, the intern should attempt to emphasize mastery of fundamentals and the practical, those areas of learning that have a clear relationship to life. Whenever possible, the "outside world" should be brought into the classroom, and frequently the classroom should find its place in the "outside world." This is not to say that certain information should never be learned for its own sake, but the student teacher should help the student relate whatever is being studied to some facet of life either inside or outside the classroom. That which is learned but is not related or used is likely to be lost soon.

Administer Diagnostic Tests.

After acquainting himself with the educational goals presented in the school system's syllabus, the intern should then prepare to administer diagnostic tests to help determine where each individual student is in his achievement and where he should be by the end of the unit. Basically, there are two types of diagnostic achievement examinations, the formal and the informal. The formal examination is designed, tested, published, and distributed by a testing company whose business it is to prepare and sell diagnostic tests for the classroom teacher. The informal diagnostic examination is designed by the classroom teacher, himself, and may take many forms. For instance, should the intern wish to find a student's general writing level, he may ask the student to write: an autobiography, answers to questions, a friendly letter, a letter to the editor of the school paper, a story, or a descriptive or expository paragraph.

What are the advantages and disadvantages of both types of diagnostic tests? The major advantage of the formal test is that when carefully chosen it may be expected to yield reliable results; its major disadvantage is its cost. The major advantages of the informal diagnostic test are that it is:

A. Inexpensive.

B. Flexible.

C. Usually reliable when carefully constructed.

D. Swift in yielding feedback.

Its major disadvantage is that the results may be unreliable if the test is not designed to yield the kind of diagnostic information being sought. Generally speaking, however, a teacher-designed diagnostic test will yield sound information that may be used to guide the intern in determining where the student is in relation to where he is expected to be at a given point in his education.

Individualize Instruction.

Upon completion of diagnostic testing and comparing where the student is with where he should be, the intern is then in a position to begin leading the individual student toward the desired instructional goals. As abilities vary, instructional goals and study materials will vary. Whenever possible, and as much as possible, individualize instruction. Remember also there must be a wide range of educational goals from grade to grade, subject to subject, and system to system.

Encourage Independent Thinking.

As well as individualizing instruction, the intern should choose with care the learning objectives for his students. Within the last decade, especially, many educators have come to see that education at all levels includes not only the learning of facts, but learning to think clearly and independently as well. Researchers and educators generally agree that all learning objectives are not of equal value in stimulating students' thinking. For instance, requiring the student to recall information demands a lower order of thinking than does the synthesizing of information, drawing generalizations from pertinent data. Beyond doubt, student teachers can lift the order of thinking in their classes by raising the levels of their learning objectives.[1]

Emphasize Higher Level Learning Objectives.

Such educators as Benjamin Bloom[2] and Ben Harris[3] have developed instruments by which learning objectives may be classified from lower to higher. Ben Harris' instrument specifies two major classes of learning objectives, cognitive and affective. There are six cognitive categories and two affective categories. The lowest cognitive learning objective is <u>recognition</u> of fact, and the highest cognitive learning objective is <u>synthesis</u> of data; the lower affective learning objective is that of <u>opinion</u>, and the higher affective learning objective is the <u>expression</u> <u>of</u> <u>deep-seated</u> <u>values</u>. Following are definitions and examples of the various levels of learning objectives.

1. *Recognition* -- The student is expected to recognize the correct option from two or more choices. <u>Examples</u>: Was Jesus Christ a Jew or an Egyptian? Was the poem "Birches" written by Robert Frost or Vachel Lindsey?

2. *Recall* -- The teacher expects the student to recall one or more simple facts. <u>Example</u>: What is one primary color?

3. *Demonstration of a skill* -- The student is expected to apply knowledge in the performance of a skill as in reading, mathematics, or language study. <u>Examples</u>: What does the first line of "Fire and Ice" say? (Word recognition). How many thirds are in a whole? (Simple arithmetic skill). Give the French translation of this English sentence. (Foreign language translation).

4. *Comprehension* -- The student demonstrates that he understands simple relations among facts. <u>Examples</u>: Give the meaning of the last stanza of "Richard Cory." (Understanding of relation among elements). Show us what you mean by an insulting gesture.

5. *Analysis* -- The student shows that he can explain an involved occurrence. <u>Examples</u>: Why did the propeller turn when we forced air through it? Explain why Oedipus continues to search for the killer of Laius after he, Oedipus, realizes that he, himself, may well be the slayer? (Explains a complex occurrence).

6. *Synthesis* -- The student is expected to combine or rearrange elements so as to develop a new generalization, arrangement, or organization. <u>Examples</u>: In view of costs of higher education, a decline in population, and an oversupply of college graduates, what would you predict the future of higher education to be during the next decade? Seeing how Oedipus becomes suddenly angry with Creon, screams at Teiresias, and threatens the herdsman, what can you conclude about one side of Oedipus' character?

Two categories of learning objectives are defined below, with examples which represent calling for affective rather than cognitive responses.

7. *Opinion* -- The student's response involves expression of feelings of personal opinion on relatively simple matters, excluding fact. <u>Examples</u>: How do you think Robert Frost's horse felt as he waited for his master, who was watching the woods fill with snow? How do you feel when you come upon an automobile accident on the highway?

8. *Attitude, or Value* -- The student is to express and defend deep-seated convictions or values. <u>Examples</u>: Do you believe in capital punishment? Why? Do you think Oedipus should have been condemned to exile or death? Why? (Deep-seated values involved).

Test Soundness Of Ideas.

In addition to designing higher level cognitive and affective learning
goals, the intern should determine to test the soundness of ideas studied in
the classroom. He, leading the class, should as a matter of practice evaluate _what_ is said, thereby assisting the students in separating the "grain"
from the "chaff," wisdom from folly. There are two major evaluative principles that the intern should encourage the pupils to use. First, the writer
(or speaker) must be factual. If the one presenting the idea is using what he
purports to be "facts" to support his conclusions, not only must the intern
assist the students in verifying these pivotal facts, but he and the pupils
must also be sure that the writer's conclusions are logically drawn from these
facts, not from bias or prejudice.

Next, every intern, as well as more mature students, should have a
philosophy of life against which he can measure a writer's or speaker's fundamental position. This philosophy of life serves as a standard, incomplete and
temporary though it is likely to be, that indicates whether or not an idea is
to be accepted or rejected. For instance, the comfortable, shallow eighteenth
century theory of philosophical optimism--the belief that whatever exists
ought to exist--was thoroughly debunked by Voltaire in _Candide_. Voltaire recognized that this quaint theory was illogical, was out of harmony with his
basic philosophic belief that both good and evil exist, and that good is
preferable to evil. Therefore, the intern, serving as a model, should always
test with the students the soundness of ideas being studied in class.

4. *CONSIDER _HOW_ TO TEACH THAT WHICH HAS BEEN SELECTED*

After the intern has analyzed the needs of his students, chosen learning
goals and materials in keeping with these needs, structured studies emphasiz-
ing fundamentals, designed higher level cognitive and affective goals for his
students, and provided for evaluating the soundness of ideas being studied,

his next major instructional decision is deciding <u>how</u> to teach effectively

that which has been chosen as being worthy of study.

When deciding <u>how</u> to teach a given "subject," the intern should have two

basic concerns: (1) the nature of the learning objectives and (2) the stu-

dents' level of mastery of that to be learned. Since the second of these two

concerns has been discussed earlier in this chapter, attention will now focus

on the first, choosing an instructional method that will complement the nature

of the learning objective.

Support Drill With A-V Aids.

If the learning objective requires the student merely to <u>recognize</u> facts

or <u>recall</u> information, the intern may choose to employ rather standard instruc-

tional methods such as drill, repetition, and association. However, using

these methods, or any methods, alone can be deadening to the point of stifling

much interest and motivation that the student may have; consequently, they

should be used in conjunction with an abundance of A-V aids such as the chalk-

board, books, filmstrips, 16mm movies, loop tapes, television, pictures, dia-

grams, graphs, and models as well as disc and tape recordings. As frequently

as possible, the students themselves should be encouraged to make and use the

A-V devices employed in the teaching-learning process.

Give Guided Practice When Teaching A Skill.

If the learning objective requires the student to demonstrate a <u>skill</u>,

practice is essential. Guided practice is, of course, preferable to unguided

practice, which may be counter productive should a student learn to perform a

skill in an inefficient way. For instance, having learned to type by the

"hunt and peck" method can put a student at a distinct disadvantage when he

begins to learn to type by the conventional, professional method, for he must

unlearn the inefficient method as well as learn the efficient one. Or, a

student, having learned to play the scale on the violin without using his little finger, will find learning to play the scale, using all four fingers, formidable, indeed. Therefore, <u>guided</u> practice from the beginning is necessary if the student is to master the skill satisfactorily with a minimum of difficulty. In addition, regular and adequate practice times are essential as is a constant monitoring of the student's progress in performing the skill in situations ranging from relaxed to tense. Feedback from the evaluation of the student's performance should then be used by the intern to determine his next instructional move.

Use Discussion In Reaching Higher Level Learning Objectives.

When choosing an instructional objective requiring more complex mental functions such as comprehension, analysis, synthesis, or evaluation, the student teacher will need to consider teaching methods which will expose the student to and give him practice in sound reasoning. In most classes at the elementary, intermediate, and high school levels, much time should be spent in class discussion, for in discussion the students are <u>actively</u> involved in the consideration and evaluation of ideas.

Lead Vigorous Discussions.

There are two basic types of discussion: teacher led and pupil led. The intern may lead class discussion in various ways. In some instances he may emphasize the use of questions.[4] At other times he may open discussion by presenting intellectually challenging films, books, poems, stories, biographies, autobiographies, essays, records, and learning tapes.

Also, the intern himself, acting as a model, can do much to encourage higher levels of thinking by his students. By objectively and accurately presenting facts and opinions of others and by showing the soundness or fallacies present in the ideas being studied, the student teacher may be a daily living illustration of how to go about drawing out truth and wisdom from a well of confusion, half-truths, error, and bias present in much thinking and writing

today. By clearly identifying, analyzing, and suggesting solutions to problems and issues of concern to his pupils, he may first show them how to
separate truth from error, fact from opinion, and then guide them as they engage in the same types of intellectual challenges.

Guide Pupils In Leading Discussions.

Pupil-led discussions may also promote higher levels of thinking in the
teaching-learning process at the upper elementary, intermediate, and high
school levels, especially when such discussion is prepared for and monitored
by the student teacher.

Plan For Students To Use All Types Of Discussion.

There are at least six major types of student-led discussions:

1. *Small Discussion Groups* - Dividing the class into small
   discussion groups to consider carefully prepared topics
   and questions on assignments may involve virtually every
   student in higher levels of mental activity. The intern,
   making certain that each group is led by a competent
   student, "floats" about the room coaching, probing, questioning, and monitoring the quantity and quality of all
   discussion.

2. *Class Discussion* - The entire class participates in
   student-led discussion, based on carefully prepared questions or carefully chosen ideas that are likely to promote
   higher levels of thinking. Although the student teacher
   will frequently prepare and select the discussion subject
   matter, at times he should allow the students to assist
   him in making such selections.

3. *Panel Discussions* - The class is divided into panels of
   four to six members. Each panel is given a set of teacher

92

or teacher-student prepared questions or topics on pre-assigned materials. The intern appoints an able student moderator, who opens, mediates, and closes the discussion. During the discussion the panel members, class members, and student teacher participate, the special role of the intern being to insure that a high level of thinking is maintained. This he may do by suggesting higher level questions,[5] following through on lower level student questions with higher level questions, providing needed information or facts, making certain that conclusions are logical outgrowths of data, and informally observing and evaluating the degree of intellectual involvement of each student.

4. *Reports* - The student teacher may assign students to present both formal and informal reports. With some direction from the intern, these may be prepared so as to stimulate the listeners to engage in higher levels of thinking, especially when the report is concluded with a discussion rising out of teacher-student prepared questions based on the information or ideas presented in the report.

5. *Debate* - Students should be encouraged to engage in debate. Generally speaking, debate is a form of oral conflict carried on in an informal or formal, highly regulated manner. Debate is valuable. It encourages higher levels of thinking, makes for leadership, promotes objectivity, and assists the student in speaking with clarity, confidence, and force. Another great value of debate is helping the student disagree congenially and respectfully with someone posing a viewpoint different from his own. When

leading students into _formal_ debate, the intern should keep in mind the following fundamental principles:

1. Choose a topic that is debatable, a topic with _one_ specific question on which there is a disagreement of opinion.

2. Take a clear position either supporting or opposing the proposition.

3. Find and focus of the main issues or contentions.

4. Develop a forceful position by using proof, which may be defined as the logical drawing of conclusions from ample, relevant evidence such as facts, statistics, examples, and quotations from authorities.

5. Anticipate and refute the arguments of the opposition by presenting facts, statistics, examples, and quotations which show that the proof is weak, the arguments irrelevant or inconsistent, the statements incorrect or deceptive, the logic unsound, or the authority unreliable.

6. Capture the audience's sympathy by appealing to their good judgement, honesty, and respect for fair play.

When guiding students into _informal_ debate, encourage them to observe the following principles:

1. Remember that the object of debate is to win the approval of the audience.

2. Develop a plan of presentation that is orderly, aggressive, and anticipates and answers objections.

3. Present a wealth of varied evidence.

4. Avoid weak logic, alienation of the audience, and positions that the debater does not believe in.

Debating teams may be chosen in several ways. First, after the question has been chosen, the students may volunteer to represent one side or the other. Also, the intern may wish to assign the students to certain teams if he knows his students well. Or, the student teacher may hold tryouts at which students spend a few minutes speaking to some phase of either side of the question.

Relate Debate And Formal Logic.

When teaching intellectually advanced students debate, the intern may, at times, wish to use formal logic to sharpen their intellectual acumen. Logic is not limited to correct reasoning in physics or philosophy only; it is right reasoning on any subject.[6] When studying formal logic in class and as a matter of historic interest, the intern may wish to give limited attention to some of Aristotle's twenty-eight types of arguments used in debate. Among these are: argument from logical separation, argument from definition of terms, and argument from motives. Or the student teacher may wish to use less cumbersome arguments generally used today such as arguments from nature, analogy, authority, and consequence. Some attention could also be given to logical patterns present in inductive and deductive reasoning. A limited amount of time might well be spent, too, on the nature of the syllogism and its use. Some high school students enjoy making a game of developing syllogisms; the classic, simple example that the intern may wish to use initially when launching a study of syllogisms is:

Major Premise: All men are subject to death.

Minor Premise: Tom is a man

95

Conclusion: Therefore, Tom is subject to death.

Explain the use of the syllogism in both inductive and deductive reasoning.

Remember, help the students to relate the study of logic to those ideas,

problems, and issues being debated in and outside the classroom.

6. *Role Playing* - This discussion technique is unrehearsed dramatization

dealing with various types of social situations or problems. To give the

students opportunity to practice adjusting to various social situations and

using the English language effectively when engaging in social intercourse,

the intern may wish frequently to guide his students into role playing. Sit-

uations which the students may wish to role play are: borrowing an item from

a friend and returning it, applying for a job, asking a friend for a date,

selling an item in a store or door-to-door, introducing oneself to a new

teacher, mailing a package at the post office, welcoming a friend into one's

home, explaining a low grade to one's parents, or thanking a host for a won-

derful evening. Also, after the students have studied a historical event, a

novel, a drama, or a short story, the class may wish to choose key scenes and

demonstrate through role playing how the major characters could have related

differently to certain problems or situations.

Ask Higher Level Questions.

Another forceful instructional tool of the intern is the question. Since

the Golden Age of Greece when Socrates challenged his students by raising and

attempting to answer questions, educators have recognized that in the instruc-

tional process questions may be of great value because of their capacity to

stimulate thinking. Since the early part of this century, especially, educa-

tors have been interested in the effectiveness of the question as a pedagogi-

cal tool. Degarmo (1889, 1911) and Betts (1911) pointed out that questions

can be used in various ways to raise the level of student thinking.[7] Burton

(1960) concluded that questions can be used in assisting students to think

96

precisely.[8] In addition, a wealth of research indicates that a high percentage of teachers use no questions or questions that demand lower levels of thinking. Flanders (1970) studied the levels of questions asked in sixteenth fourth grade classes studying a unit on social studies and summarized his findings by noting that the proportion of questions concerned with higher levels of think-ing, inductive and deductive reasoning, synthesizing, and generalizing," probably reaches an incidence that is below 15 or even 10 percent during sub-ject matter discussion."[9] Hevener (1973), studying the questioning patterns of student teachers of literature, found that approximately one-fourth of the interns asked no questions and that approximately two-thirds of the student teachers' questions was at the lower cognitive and lower affective levels.[10]

One of the most striking statements about the values of questioning in instruction comes from Postman and Weingartner:

> Knowledge is produced in response to questions. And new knowl-edge results from the asking of new questions about old questions. Here is the point: Once you have learned how to ask questions -- relevant and appropriate and substantial questions -- you have learned how to learn and no one can keep you from learning whatever you want or need to know .... The most important intellectual ability man has yet developed (is) the art...of asking questions.[11]

If to "question well is to teach well,"[12] one of the most reliable ways for the student teacher to stimulate thinking is for him to ask questions that will call forth higher levels of intellectual activity (comprehension, analy-sis, synthesis, and value responses), discussed earlier in this chapter.

5. *PLAN ALL INSTRUCTION*

Effective teaching also requires careful planning. The student teacher needs to engage in three levels of planning. First, he develops broad learn-ing objectives, discussed earlier in this chapter. Next, he divides the broad learning objectives into units. Finally, he breaks the units into seg-ments, and a daily lesson plan is developed around each segment.

Develop Units.

A unit of study may vary in length from a few days to a few months. Normally, several units will be studied during a grading period, with the final unit being concluded just before the students are to receive their report cards, report sheets, or other forms of evaluation for that grading period.

Plan Units Around Selected Subjects.

Units may be based on limited or broad subjects. A unit may be developed around such topics as: one person; an organization; a city, state or nation; a discovery; an experiment; a literary, musical or art form; a historic event; or a social phenomenon.

Select Learning Activities.

The intern may include in his units such learning activities as: conducting school or community polls; writing and producing video and radio programs; writing reports, short stories, poems, autobiographies, biographies, and songs; making booklets; reading, carrying on class discussion and panel discussions; giving oral reports; taking field trips; performing; constructing models; listening to resource persons from the community; and evaluating movies as well as TV and radio programs. Remember, learning is likely to be most effective when the students are <u>actively</u> <u>engaged</u> in activities related to the learning goals.

Outline The Unit.

When outlining a unit of study, the intern should include:

I.   Profile of students.
    A.   Chronological age-range of class.
    B.   Mental age-range of class.

II. Relationship of unit to long range learning objectives.
    A.   Specifically state the long-range learning objectives.
    B.   Show how the unit fits into these long-range objectives.
    C.   When possible, state unit objectives in behavioral terms.

III. Content
   A. State the subject matter to be learned.
   B. State the skills to be mastered.
   C. State the problems to be solved.
   D. State the experiences to be undergone.
   E. State the levels of thinking to be employed.

IV. Methods
   A. State the activities to be engaged in by the student.
   B. State the activities to be engaged in by the intern.
   C. State the activities to be engaged in by the others, such as community resource persons.

V. Materials
   A. List visual and sound materials to be used.
   B. List printed materials to be used.
   C. Indicate where all needed materials are located.
   D. Indicate when all needed materials are available.

VI. Review
   A. Show how all studies will be reviewed.

VII. Evaluation
   A. Show how you will measure the students' level of mastery at the beginning of the unit.
   B. Show how you will measure the students' achievement in subject matter, skills, problem solving, experiences gained, and levels of thinking at the end of the unit.

Develop Lesson Plans.

After the unit has been planned, the student teacher should develop daily lesson plans. Lesson plans are valuable because they: (1) force the intern to review the major learning objectives, (2) require him to state the specific learning objective, (3) encourage him to relate each day's activity to the previous day's assignment, (4) require him to break down the specific learning objective into smaller goals, (5) force him to show how the learning objectives are to be reached, (6) encourage him to assess daily student progress, (7) encourage him to summarize and review what has been learned that day, (8) assist him in preparing an assignment in keeping with the major and specific learning objectives,[13] (9) and require him to identify and locate the materials he will need when teaching the lesson.

Although daily lesson plan formats differ, the following skeletal sample may be considered typical.[14]

Date: <u>Day</u>, <u>Month</u>, <u>Year</u>

Class <u>9th Grade English</u>

Major Objectives: <u>Students are to be able to read and interpret sonnets</u>
<u>and recognize sonnet forms.</u>

Specific Objective: <u>Students are to be able to read, recognize, and</u>
<u>interpret English sonnets.</u>

Review: <u>Review material studied during previous class period.</u>

Specific Learning Goals	Method
1. Read sonnets 2. Recognize Shakespeare's Sonnets 153 and 154 as English sonnet 3. Identify rhyme scheme 4. Identify number of lines 5. Identify closing couplets 6. Interpret sonnets	1. Teacher will use filmstrip explaining structure of English sonnet. 2. Teacher will call on students to read Sonnet 153 and 154. 3. Teacher will put rhyme scheme of sonnet 153 on board. Students will identify rhyme scheme of sonnet 154 on handout; teacher will lead discussion. 4. Teacher will point out number of lines in sonnets 153 and 154. 5. Teacher will identify couplet in 153; students will identify couplet in 154. 6. Teacher will lead discussion of Sonnet 153; selected student will lead discussion of Sonnet 154.

Summary: Have students state major points they have learned.

Assignment: Write an English sonnet (or) choose one of Shakespeare's sonnets,
interpret its meaning, and explain why you agree or disagree with
what the author is saying.

Materials: Filmstrip, projector, sonnet handout.

Be Prepared To Adjust Lesson Plans.

Remember that lesson plans are tentative and that unexpected occurrences may prompt a change in the very best plans. For example, the students may advance more slowly or rapidly than anticipated, or a given teaching technique may not be working. In either event, the intern would need to make adjustments not reflected in his daily lesson plans. The tail (lesson plans) should not be allowed to wag the dog (students' instructional needs).

Prepare Lesson Plans Early.

The intern should make up lesson plans at least one week in advance so that he will have a clear overview of the subject matter to be studied the ensuing week. Also, during a given class period, if the class should finish studying the planned subject matter early, the intern could go immediately to an introduction of the topic to be engaged in the next day.

Make Assignments.

The assignment, an indispensable instructional tool when properly employed, should be: (1) related to the general and specific learning objectives, (2) challenging but not too difficult, (3) vital and interesting, (4) of appropriate length, (5) and clearly stated. The students should know exactly <u>what</u> is expected of them, <u>what</u> the purpose of the assignment is, and <u>how</u> the assignment is to be executed. The assignment should be given before the end of the period so that the students have opportunity to ask questions about any part that they find unclear. Students should know that their assigned work will be reviewed and responded to by the intern and/or classmates. If this is not done, the students will feel that because the intern does not take assignments seriously, neither should they be expected to do so.

Assignments can provide valuable instructional information by indicating to the intern such data as: the student's ability to work independently, his degree of love for learning, his level of mastery of basic skills such as

101

reading, comprehension, writing, and maturity of judgment, and his ability to follow instructions.

6. *CAREFULLY SELECT A-V AIDS*

As has been discussed earlier in this chapter, the intern may add interest, sparkle, and appeal to his instruction by carefully choosing appropriate audio and visual aids.

Use The Blackboard.

Of all such aids, the blackboard, or chalkboard, is probably the most valuable. It is always present, always convenient, inexpensive, easily cleared for fresh use, large, and adaptable. The following suggestions will make for effective instructional use of the blackboard:

1. At the end of each day, see that the blackboard is clean for the next day's classes.

2. Frequently change the decorations over the blackboard.

3. Don't be afraid to doodle as you talk; writing key words and drawing rough diagrams on the board add interest and clarity to most classroom presentations and discussions.

4. Use a high grade chalk that makes a distinct, firm mark.

5. Keep erasers clean.

6. Make all writing large and legible.

7. Make all visual designs large and distinct.

8. When discussing the writing or illustrations, stand beside the material.

9. Adjust the blinds if there is a glare on the board.

10. Don't erase the writing too quickly; give the students ample opportunity to study the material.

11. Don't crowd the illustrations and writing.

12. If you have a lot of writing to display, whenever possible, put it on the board before class begins.

13. Frequently use colored chalk to: contrast points, add, interest, emphasize key words and show divisions.

14. Frequently allow students to work at the board.

Use The Bulletin Board.

The bulletin board, as well, may be a forceful instructional tool by attractively presenting information, offering thought-provoking concepts, and encouraging students to pursue various facets of learning. The ensuing suggestions will go far in making bulletin boards of the greatest instructional value:

1. Make the bulletin board colorful, neat, aesthetically balanced, and three dimensional.

2. Give each display <u>one</u> clear message.

3. Actively involve the viewer by having him name some object (answer wheel, answer cards, pointer, etc.) of the display.

4. Encourage the viewer to pursue the theme by directing him to books, charts, displays, etc.

5. Whenever possible in each display use at least one "real" key object (butterfly, booklet, map, stone, carving, string, etc.).

6. Display students' work.

7. Make the "message" short and direct.

8. Choose a theme in keeping with subject matter being studied in class.

9. When designing the bulletin board, keep in mind the level of maturity of the viewers.

10. Frequently allow students to create bulletin board displays.

11. To maintain student interest in the bulletin board, see that the displays are changed frequently.

7. EVALUATE EACH STUDENT'S PERFORMANCE WITH CARE

Another major instructional matter to which the student teacher must give earnest attention is the evaluation of the student's work. Interns discover that assigning a grade is difficult because it involves judgment, and judging (evaluating) may well be the most challenging intellectual activity of man.

Design Testing Criteria.

When designing grading criteria, the intern must consider such questions as: (1) What is an unacceptable level of performance? (2) What is the minimal level of acceptable performance? (3) What is an "average" level of performance? and (4) What is a superior level of performance? There is no neatly packaged answer to these difficult questions; when answering them the student teacher should take into consideration: (1) the student's level of mastery of the concerned information or skill when he began the study, (2) his intellectual capacity, (3) his level of dedication and effort, (4) his progress, (5) his social background, and (6) his ability to meet the demands of the next step in the learning process.

Allow For Flexibility In Grading.

Therefore, because of the many variables which need to be taken into consideration, grading criteria should afford the intern flexibility, allowing him to take into account individual differences. When assigning a grade, the student teacher strives for <u>fairness</u>, and fairness requires that individual differences and abilities be considered. Consequently, the <u>good</u> <u>judgment</u> and <u>wisdom</u> of the intern is taxed fully when he is faced with the issuing of grades.

8. REPORT ON THE STUDENT'S WORK

After evaluating the student's performance, the intern must then report on that performance to both the student and the parents.

Offer An Analysis Of The Student's Work.

Each time the intern returns an evaluated paper to the student, the paper should also include a brief analysis of the <u>strengths</u> and <u>weaknesses</u> of the paper and <u>suggestions</u> that will help the student to see how he can successfully meet his particular problems.

104

Give Early Feedback.

In addition, evaluated papers should be returned to the student as early as possible, for early feedback takes advantage of student interest and assures the student that he will be able to take full advantage of corrective suggestions before he is required to do another similar assignment.

Give Balanced Feedback.

When the student teacher is reporting on the student's performance at the end of a marking period, the semester, or the academic year, he should, as time allows, include not only a "letter grade" and a "form evaluation," but also a specific, concise, clearly written statement including observations on the student's initiative, attitude toward learning, degree of academic progress, and level of mastery of the subject.

Keep Parents Informed.

Also, as soon as the intern suspects that a student may receive a failing grade for a marking period, he should notify in writing the student's parents of this possibility. Frequently, such a note will cause indifferent parents to encourage their child to put forth more effort to learn. In addition, the notice, a physical reminder that a failing grade is a distinct possibility, may encourage the talented but lazy student to mend his ways. The note, brief, courteous, and factual, should be mailed to the parents and a carbon copy retained in the student teacher's files.

Be Prompt With Grades.

At the end of a marking period, the intern makes certain that he is prepared to distribute grades on the day set by the school. On that day the intern usually gives the "report cards" to the students at the end of the school day in the elementary school and at the end of the appropriate class period in secondary schools.

Confer With Parents.

With the report cards, the intern should distribute a schedule of times when the parents may make appointments to discuss the student's progress, achievement, and needs. Times for these appointments are usually scheduled for the late afternoon or early evening. For the convenience of the parents who wish to schedule conferences, the intern should include his phone number and when he can be reached. Or, the student teacher himself may wish to take the initiative in scheduling conferences with some parents. After the conference has been scheduled, the intern should:

1.   Arrange for a comfortable, private conference room.

2.   Be friendly and courteous when greeting the parents.

3.   Review the student's progress with the parents.

4.   Review the student's problems with the parents.

5.   Make specific recommendations concerning how the student may successfully meet his problems.

6.   Suggest ways for the parents to help the student.

7.   Allow the parents to talk.

8.   Encourage the parents to ask questions.

9.   If another conference is advisable, arrange for it.

10. Thank the parents for their time and interest.

11. End the conference on a friendly, positive note.

Use Grades To Assist In Instructional Planning.

The intern should recognize that grades are not for the benefit of the student and the parent only. Grades also assist the student teacher in instructional planning. By keeping careful records of the progress of an individual student or an entire class, the intern has available pertinent information which can direct him in his next instructional move. On the basis of carefully analyzing test results, the intern may decide to make adjustments in his broad instructional objectives, his unit plans, his daily lesson plans, or his instructional objectives for individual students.

[1]Fillmer Hevener, Jr., The Types of Oral Questions Asked by Student Teachers of Literature at the Eighth, Ninth, and Tenth Grade Levels, University Microfilms, U. Michigan, 1973.

[2]Benjamin Bloom, Taxonomy of Educational Objectives (New York: Longmans, Green, and Co., 1956).

[3]Benjamin Harris, In-Service Education (New Jersey: Prentice-Hall, Inc., 1969), pp. 154-155.

[4]Later in this chapter further consideration is given to the use of questions in teaching.

[5]Higher level questions require such mental skills as comprehension, analysis, synthesis, and evaluation.

[6]Richard Hughes and P. A. Duhamel, Rhetoric (New Jersey: Prentice-Hall, Inc., 1962), 6.

[7]Francis P. Hunkins, "Analysis and Evaluation Questions: Their Effects Upon Critical Thinking," Educational Leadership, (April, 1970), 697-705.

[8]Hunkins, loc. cit.

[9]Ned Flanders, Analyzing Teaching Behavior) Reading, Mass. Addison Wesley Publishing Co., 1970), 299.

[10]Hevener, loc. cit., pp. 66-69.

[11]Neil Postman and Charles Weingartner, Teaching As a Subversive Activity (New York: Decarte Press, 1969), 23.

[12]R. L. Laughlin, "On Questioning," The Educational Forum, 25 (May, 1961), 481.

[13]For an example of major and specific learning objectives, see the sample lesson plan which immediately follows.

[14]For alternant lesson plan model, see Glossary B.

CHAPTER 12

BEING A PROFESSIONAL

When beginning the student teaching practicum, the intern becomes a professional, joining some 2,130,000 other elementary and secondary teachers in the United States. As a professional, the student teacher must display unquestioned ability in pedagogy, generally, but he must do much more. He must earn the respect of his students, his colleagues, his supervisors, and the public at large by reason of his professional education, his competence, and his educational leadership.

1. *BE DEDICATED*

The professional teacher should show absolute dedication to the pursuit and dissemination of truth. He should serve with boundless enthusiasm, always being ready to assist both students and administrators, to go the "second mile" no matter how personally inconvenient this may be. Even though such dedication is not always found in the teaching profession, the intern should not allow himself to use such a lack to serve as an excuse for slack service. *Lift The Professional Image.*

When serving others with competence and devotion, the intern lifts his own professional image. At the same time he assists in lifting the professional image of the entire teaching profession.

2. *OBSERVE PROFESSIONAL PRACTICES*

As well as being dedicated to his profession, the student teacher should be aware of and observe certain basic professional practices. *Do Not Divulge Confidential Information.*

Although the intern has full access to student files, he should use these files only when seeking information that will aid him in better serving the student professionally. The student teacher should never explore a student's file out of mere curiosity or a desire to gather damaging information. All personal data about students should be held in the strictest confidence. When appropriate, the intern may offer personal information about a student to administrators, fellow-teachers, and the parents of the student; such information, however, should never be given to others who have no direct professional or parental involvement.

Handle Human Relations Problems With Care.

Furthermore, should the student teacher feel that he has been wronged by a colleague (be he teacher or administrator), the intern should first go directly to the alleged offender and attempt to resolve the matter. If resolution at this level cannot be realized, the intern may then wish to take the case to higher school authorities. Never, however, should a student teacher discuss such a conflict with students or their parents.

Give Attention To Personal Matters.

In addition, as is discussed in detail in Chapter VI, the professional teacher needs to be punctual, to make himself available for student and parent conferences, to keep himself well groomed, and to display good taste in dress.

Study Professional Literature.

Also, as is observed in Chapter V, the student teaching practicum is an excellent time to become acquainted with and begin the practice of regularly reading professional educational journals, for, as intern or full-time teacher, the alert professional needs to be aware of the latest developments, research, and trends in education.

Be Prepared To Handle "Crushes."

Because interns are normally youthful, ranging in age from the late teens to the early twenties, it is not unusual for the more mature male high school student to have a "crush" on the female intern. Although it is considered un-professional for the intern to date her students, she should be extremely careful not to offend the enamored student. The student teacher may explain in kind, polite, clear terms that her refusal is based, not on a personal dis-like for the student, but on the professional principle that interns do not date their students. An intern dating a student would run the risk of having the enamored student exaggerate to his fellow students how he "made-out with the teacher last night." In addition, she may wish to explain to her would-be suitor that a conflict of interest would be involved since it would, no doubt, be impossible for her, the teacher, to <u>objectively</u> evaluate the quality of the work of the student whom she is dating.

Allow Time For Recreation.

On the other hand, the student teacher should feel perfectly free to socialize. Even though interning is demanding, the student teacher needs to vary his activities, to spice his work with a dash of recreation and relaxa-tion. All work and no play still makes "Ivan, the intern," an insipid in-structor.

Properly Represent The Profession At All Times.

The student teacher should remember that he is at <u>all</u> <u>times</u> representing the teaching profession, whether he be in the classroom or in the community. Consequently, the intern should conduct himself with the same degree of propriety when away from school that he displays when in the classroom. Re-member, the title <u>teacher</u> carries with it both <u>honor</u> and <u>responsibility</u>.

Refrain From Engaging In Other Work.

Because student teaching is a <u>full-time</u> job requiring enormous amounts of time as well as intellectual and nervous energy, the intern should avoid en-gaging in any other work without the express consent of: the college director of student teaching, the college student teaching counselor, and the supervising teacher. Even if these persons should agree to a schedule allowing a very limited amount of additional part-time work, for his own protection, the intern should never engage in other employment to an extent that is likely to affect his pedagogical proficiency. Except in very rare instances involving extreme financial exigencies, the intern should not engage in work beyond his student teaching.

3. *KEEP A HIGH MORALE*

Don't forget that people aren't perfect, and because schools are made up of people, schools aren't perfect. Once the student teacher is on the inside of the educational organization, he will find some people and some practices that leave much to be desired. The intern may discover that:

a. Administrators have "pets."

b. Colleagues are jealous of his quality teaching.

c. Experienced teachers resent his suggestions.

d. He is ignored or avoided if he belongs to a minority race, religion, or political party.

e. He is put under pressure to join certain "professional" organizations whose goals, political or otherwise, he does not wish to support.

f. He is given an unequal work load.

g. His colleagues smile to his face and attack behind his back.

h. His colleagues gloat over his professional problems.

i. He is almost never thanked for his services.

j. His failures, not his successes, are dwelt upon by his colleagues.

Remember, however, that not all educators are like this. Many are truly generous, fair, understanding, appreciative, and kind. Looking at these and modeling himself after them, the student teacher is able to keep his faith in man, educators, and the educational system. In short, he <u>can</u> <u>keep</u> his morale high.

4. *ENGAGE IN SELF EXAMINATION*

It was Socrates who taught that "the unexamined life is not worth living." Paraphrasing Socrates, one might conclude that unexamined teaching is not worthy of the name. The professional teacher should frequently review his professional performance; the following instrument will serve as a guide in the self-appraisal process.

Indicate your self-evaluation on each item by placing a circle around the appropriate number. If, upon evaluating yourself, you are dissatisfied with your performance in any area, resolve to do your best to improve. Check yourself frequently!

I. <u>Instructional Preparation.</u>   <u>Low</u>   <u>High</u>

1. Am I aware of the latest research   1 2 3 4 5
    and professional opinion in my field?

2. Have I mastered the subject matter   1 2 3 4 5
    of each unit?

3. Have I organized each lesson and   1 2 3 4 5
    each unit of study?

4. Have I clearly defined the instructional   1 2 3 4 5
    objective for each lesson and unit?

5. Have I prepared and/or selected appropriate   1 2 3 4 5
    instructional materials for each lesson
    and unit?

6. Am I able to show relationships between   1 2 3 4 5
    disciplines?

II. <u>Instructional Methods</u>.

		<u>Low</u>				<u>High</u>
7.	Do I individualize instruction as much as possible?	1	2	3	4	5
8.	Am I aware of the abilities of each student?	1	2	3	4	5
9.	Do I briefly review the previous day's work with the class?	1	2	3	4	5
10.	Do I attempt to make the classroom attractive and comfortable?	1	2	3	4	5
11.	Do I create a relaxed atmosphere conducive to learning?	1	2	3	4	5
12.	Do I frequently use questions that encourage comprehension, analysis, synthesis, and evaluation?	1	2	3	4	5
13.	Do I often involve the students in learning activities?	1	2	3	4	5
14.	Do I use a variety of teaching methods?	1	2	3	4	5
15.	Do I use a variety of teaching materials?	1	2	3	4	5
16.	Do I praise students when they show progress?	1	2	3	4	5.
17.	Do I increase the student's interest in learning?	1	2	3	4	5
18.	Do I use appropriate A-V aids?	1	2	3	4	5
19.	Do I make clear explanations?	1	2	3	4	5
20.	Do I draw upon community resources?	1	2	3	4	5
21.	Do I make use of diagnostic and achievement tests?	1	2	3	4	5
22.	Do I relate what is being studied to some part of life?	1	2	3	4	5
23.	Am I able to hold the interest of the class?	1	2	3	4	5

24. Do I give clear assignments?   1 2 3 4 5

25. Do I know and use students' names?   1 2 3 4 5

26. Do I encourage independent study?   1 2 3 4 5

27. Is my word choice on an appropriate level?   1 2 3 4 5

28. Am I available for parent and student conferences?   1 2 3 4 5

III. Human Relations.

29. Do I avoid embarrassing students?   1 2 3 4 5

30. Do I allow all students to be heard?   1 2 3 4 5

31. Do I praise colleagues for their accomplishments?   1 2 3 4 5

32. Do I respect confidentiality?   1 2 3 4 5

33. Do I sympathize with those in need?   1 2 3 4 5

34. Do I avoid engaging in gossip about colleagues?   1 2 3 4 5

35. Do I refrain from interfering in professional   1 2 3 4 5

matters that are not my responsibility?

36. Do I avoid criticizing a colleague?   1 2 3 4 5

37. Do I forgive?   1 2 3 4 5

38. Do I follow the "chain of command? when making   1 2 3 4 5

a complaint?

39. Am I cooperative?   1 2 3 4 5

40. Am I courteous?   1 2 3 4 5

41. Am I tactful when correcting students?   1 2 3 4 5

42. Am I fair to everyone?   1 2 3 4 5

43. Do I respect the views of all persons?   1 2 3 4 5

44. Do I refrain from holding grudges?   1 2 3 4 5

IV. Personal Qualities.

45. Am I honest?   1 2 3 4 5

46. Am I reliable?   1 2 3 4 5

		Low				High
47.	Do I dress neatly?	1	2	3	4	5
48.	Do I dress appropriately?	1	2	3	4	5
49.	Do I cultivate my voice to be pleasant, clear, and forceful?	1	2	3	4	5
50.	Do I care for my health?	1	2	3	4	5
51.	Am I poised and at ease when teaching?	1	2	3	4	5
52.	Am I enthusiastic?	1	2	3	4	5
53.	Am I self-directing?	1	2	3	4	5
54.	Do I have a sense of humor?	1	2	3	4	5
55.	Am I willing to accept corrective, objective suggestions?	1	2	3	4	5
56.	Am I a model citizen?	1	2	3	4	5
57.	Do I support worthy community activities?	1	2	3	4	5
58.	Do I think before acting?	1	2	3	4	5
59.	Is my judgment sound?	1	2	3	4	5
60.	Am I punctual?	1	2	3	4	5
61.	Am I independent in my thinking?	1	2	3	4	5

The intern who follows professional practices will gain the respect of students, parents, faculty, and administrators.

THE END

116

GLOSSARY A

TWENTY-NINE "ONE LINERS": ADVICE FROM SUCCESSFUL STUDENT TEACHERS

1. Don't be afraid; smile and be yourself always.

2. <u>All</u> beginning teachers should take at least one course in the teaching of reading before going out to teach.

3. Have confidence in yourself; you are capable of teaching successfully.

4. Take time to analyze your honest feelings about choosing teaching as a career; it's your life that will be spent in the classroom.

5. Remember, respect is a two-way street.

6. The secret of successful student teaching is remembering that you are a guest in another teacher's classroom.

7. Above all, when you are discouraged, don't lose your sense of perspective; brighter days are ahead.

8. If you wish to be appreciated by your students, you must be firm, but kind, from the very first day.

9. Establish rapport with the college supervisor and the supervising teacher; develop a close working relationship with both.

10. Never assume that your students know anything, whether the material in question was taught by another teacher or yourself.

11. Remember to keep a smile on your face because students tend to act the way you are acting; be enthusiastic and willing to show them that you are there to make learning fun and worthwhile.

12. Be prepared to learn from your students.

13. Broaden your experiences so that you can help broaden the experiences of your students.

14. Always go into the classroom prepared.

15. Never be afraid to say, "I don't know the answer, but I'll try to find it."

16. Since students are human, they need recognition.

17. Much satisfaction may be gained from student teaching, but don't expect to work miracles with all students in eight or ten weeks.

18. The secret of being a successful student teacher lies in two words: "discipline" and "planning."

19. Assert yourself as leader of the classroom from the very beginning.

20. Go into student teaching with a willingness to learn as well as a want to teach.

21. Remember, if you wish to do a good job, your supervising teacher will always help you.

22. Be flexible!

23. Be fair to all students.

24. Don't enter student teaching with a negative attitude, for the students can sense your apprehension, and your worst fears could possibly come true.

25. Seek guidance from your college supervisor.

26. Don't go into the classroom as a dictator.

27. Be natural and relaxed.

28. Be your students' friend, but expect obedience.

29. Don't be overly worried about college supervisors and supervising teachers; instead, work to the best of your ability for the students, for it is here that you will find the greatest reward.

GLOSSARY B

MODEL LESSON PLAN

Class: 10th Grade (average)

Date:

General Objective: The student will identify Haiku as a form of poetry.

Specific Instructional Objectives

The Student Will:

1. Define poetry: Poetry is words chosen and arranged to create a specific intellectual or emotional response through sound, rhythm, and symbolism, especially.

2. Identify Haiku as poetry; it has sound, rhythm, and meaning. It may also have rhyme, alliteration, and assonance.

3. Identify Haiku's specific characteristics:

    A. Three lines

    B. Seventeen syllables

    C. Nature/experience themes

    D. What, when, where

Procedures

The Teacher Will:

1. Offer definition of poetry.

2. Provide examples of Haiku in a slide/tape presentation.

3. Lead discussion of Haiku based on the examples.

4. Note points of historic and structural significance.

5. Note some famous Haiku poets:

    Otsuji

    Shiki

    Issa

    Buson

questions often answered

Evaluation: Evaluate the student's level of learning by assessing his understanding as it is reflected in his oral observations about Haiku and by the written example produced by the student (see the assignment below).

Assignment: Write an original Haiku poem based on a picture of your choice; if you wish, draw or paint your own picture. Be prepared to share your creation(s) with the class tomorrow.

Examples of Haiku Poetry:

1. The spring day closes,

    Lingering

    Where there is water. -- Issa

2. A small garden

    Brimming with dew,

    Half a gallon of it. -- Shiki

3. Clearing up in the evening;

    In the pale blue sky

    Row upon row of autumn mountains. -- Issa

Sources:

Okuma, Kotomichi. A Grass Path. Honolulu: University of Hawaii Press, 1955.

Price, Dorothy, Ed. Reflections. U.S.A.: Hallmark Cards, Inc.

Yasuda, Kenneth. The Japanese Haiku. Rutland, Vermont: Charles E. Tuttle Co., 1965.

GLOSSARY C

DEFINITIONS OF KEY TERMS

Affective. That which results from feeling rather than from thought.

Attitude. One's mental state or feeling toward something or someone.

Authoritanianism. The belief that the teacher should control the classroom
    with autocratic authority.

Classroom Manager. The one designated to direct learning in the classroom.

Cluster. To put in a group.

Cognitive. That which results from thought, not feeling.

College Consultant. The representative from the subject matter department of
    the college at which the secondary student teacher is enrolled.

College Counselor. A broad term including both the college supervisor and the
    college consultant.

College Supervisor. The representative from the department of education of
    the college at which the student teacher is enrolled.

Debate. A form of oral conflict carried on in an informal or formal manner.

Deduction. An argument moving from a general observation to a limited,
    specific conclusion.

Diagnostic Test. A test designed to reveal the instructional needs of the
    student.

Discipline. Guidance designed to train students in desired conduct or action.

Disciplined Classroom. A classroom in which the teacher develops an
    atmosphere that promotes desired learning.

Educational Goals. Learning or skills to be mastered by the student.

Feedback. Information, ideas, or feelings returned by the student to the teacher.

Formal Achievement Test. A standardized achievement test developed and
distributed by a testing organization.

Formal Report. A report fully written out in advance and read to the
listeners.

Individualized Instruction. Instruction which is adapted to the specific
needs of individual students.

Induction. An argument moving from the observing of individual occurrences
to a decision regarding what all these occurrences have in common.

Informal Achievement Test. An achievement test designed by the classroom
teacher for testing specific students in his classes.

Informal Report. A report which the student presents from notes.

Intern. A student teacher; one who is practice-teaching under the supervision
of professional educators.

Learning. Knowledge acquired by formal or informal means for application in
life.

Lesson Plan. A plan for a limited topic of study usually completed in one
class period.

Libertarianism. The belief that the teacher should exert little or no re-
straint on student activity in the classroom.

Major Disciplinary Problems. Those human relations problems which normally
may not be solved by the student teacher, himself, within the classroom.

Marking Period. A designated period of time (usually six to eight weeks)
during which the student's work is evaluated and at the end of which a
final grade is given.

Master Teacher. The high school teacher under whom the student teacher interns; the supervising teacher.

Minor Disciplinary Problems. Those human relations problems which normally may be solved by the student teacher, himself, within the classroom.

Motivation. The desire to learn.

Outside World. Those areas of life beyond the four walls of the school
building.

Play. Enjoyable mental or physical activity.

Proof. The logical drawing of conclusions from ample, relevant evidence.

Role Playing. A discussion technique based on dramatization dealing with
various types of social situations or problems.

Seating Chart. A diagram which shows where each student sits and which
facilitates the taking of the roll and the learning of students' names.

Selah. A term occurring frequently in the Psalms; probably a direction from
the leader to raise the voice or to pause.

Skill. An ability coming from practice or aptitude.

Subject. An area of learning chosen to be considered, discussed, or investi-
gated.

Supervising Teacher. The high school teacher under whom the student teacher
interns; the master teacher.

Syllogism. A form of logic containing a major premise, a minor premise, and a
conclusion.

Unit. A plan for a broad topic which may be studied for several days or weeks.

Wisdom. The judicious application of knowledge.

Work. A duty or task.

BIBLIOGRAPHY

Abruscato, J. "College Supervisor of Student Teachers." Improving College and University Teaching, 20 (Spring 1972), 146, 147.

Adams-Webber, J. and E. Mir. "Assessing the Development of Student Teachers' Role Conceptions." The British Journal of Educational Psychology, 46 (November 1976), 338-340.

Alexander, R. H. "How To Prevent the Student Teaching Blues." Journal of Health, Physical Education, and Recreation, 41 (March 1970), 93-95.

Armstrong, D. G. "Equipping Student Teachers to Deal With Classroom Control Problems." The High School Journal, 60 (October 1976), 1-9.

Ashton-Warner, Sylvia. Teacher. New York: Bantam, 1971.

Barufaldi, J. P. and S. M. Hord. "Learning To Teach and Teaching to Learn." School Science and Mathematics, 77 (April 1977), 287-290.

Breiter, J. C. "Measured Self-Actualization and Student Teacher Effectiveness." Improving College and University Teaching, 18 (Winter 1975), 16-18.

Brembeck, Cole S. and T. J. Thompson. New Strategies for Educational Development. Massachusetts: Lexington Books, 1974.

Burns, Paul C. and Daniel H. Brown. The Student Teacher Evaluates Pupil Progress. Association for Student Teaching, 1962. (Bulletin #19).

Campbell, L. P. and J. A. Williamson. "Achievement Beyond Expectation." Educational Forum, 37 (March, 1973), 362.

Cappa, D. "Inexperienced Teacher and Discipline." Improving College and University Teaching, 18 (Spring 1970), 148-149.

Cohen, J. "Other Side of the Desk." College English, 35 (December 1973), 292.

Cohen, L. "Dogmatism and Views of the Ideal Pupil; Study of Mature Student Teachers." Educational Review, 24 (February 1977), 120-122.

Conforti, J. M. "Socialization of Teachers: A Case Study." Theory Into Practice, 15 (December 1976), 352-359.

Cross, J. S. and J. M. Nagle. "Supervisory Strategies For Helping Teachers Improve Students' Thinking Skills." Peabody Journal of Education, 47 (January 1970), 208-215.

Davis, B. "On Student Teaching." Media and Methods, 13 (April 1977), 50, 51.

Davis, M. D. "Eight Weeks Versus Sixteen Weeks of Student Teaching." The Journal of Educational Research, 70 (September 1976), 31-34.

Denton, J. J. and Others. "Pupil Perceptions of A Student Teacher's Competence." The Journal of Educational Research, 70 (March 1977), 180-185.

Ediger, M. "From Textbooks To Teaching." School and Community, 59 (December 1972), 11.

Ellenburg, F. C. "Discussion Topics For Evaluating Time." Instructor, 86 (October 1976), 83.

Funkhouser, C. W. "Evaluating Student Teachers." School and Community, 63 (March 1977), 13.

Garvey, R. "Self-Concept and Success In Student Teaching." The Journal of Teacher Education, 21 (Fall 1970), 357-361.

George, B. "Open Letter to the Beginning Student Teacher." Journal of Health, Physical Education, and Recreation, 43 (November 1972), 10.

Hagen, L. B. "A College Supervisor Talks To A Student Teacher." Improving College and University Teaching, 20 (Spring 1972), 161-163.

Harris, D. "Rewarding Yet Anxious." Instructor, 83 (October 1973), 31.

Heffner, C. P. "Student As Teacher." Theory Into Practice, 13 (December 1974), 371-375.

Henson, K. T. "Student Teachers Unlock Learning Barriers." School and Community, 56 (February 1970), 36.

Higgins, J. E. "Trouble With Harry." Contemporary Education, 47 (Summer 1976), 241-243.

Hoy, W. K. and R. Rees. "Bureaucratic Socialization of Student Teachers." The Journal of Teacher Education, 28 (January 1977), 23-26.

Jeffreys, Montagu Vaughan Castelman. Education: Its Nature and Purpose. New York: Barnes and Noble, 1971.

Johnson, J. S. "Student Teacher As Self." The Education Digest, 42 (May 1977), 28-31.

Jones, R. C. "University Supervisor: A Student Teacher's Best Friend." The Clearing House, 44 (March 1970), 433-436.

Kazlov, G. "Whatever Happened To The Clinical Professor?" The Journal of Teacher Education, 27 (Winter 1976), 340, 341.

Kraft, R. E. "Analysis of Supervision/Student Teacher Interaction." Journal of Health, Physical Education, and Recreation, 45 (March 1974), 37, 38.

Lindman, M. R. and G. P. Grimes. "Development and Use of Behavioral Objectives In Student Teaching." Art Education, 26 (November 1973), 11-15.

Lowther, M. A. "Successful and Unsuccessful Experiences of Student Teachers in Secondary Education." Contemporary Education, 41 (May 1970), 272-275.

MacDonald, J. B. and E. Zaret. "Student Teaching: Benefit or Burden?" The Journal of Teacher Education, 22 (Spring 1971), 51-58.

Meyer, D. E. "Student Teaching: Opportunity or Ordeal?" The Clearing House, 50 (February 1977), 258-259.

McAteer, J. F. "Student Teaching Supervision: Roles and Routines." The Clearing House, 50 (December 1976), 161-165.

Murov, R. "Awareness and Student Teaching." New York State Education, 57 (February 1970), 29.

Neal, Charles D. and Others. The Beginning Teacher at Work. Minneapolis: Burgess Publishing Co., 1971.

Needham, D. "Learning Connections: Teacher, Student Teacher, Child." Teacher, 94 (September 1976), 80-83.

Ogletree, J. "My Student Teaching Experience." Journal of Health, Physical Education, and Recreation, 43 (April 1972), 29.

Pearson, N. P. Instructional Materials Centers. Minneapolis: Burgess Publishing Co., 1971.

Peter, W. G. "10 Commandments For Student Teachers." School and Community, 61 (October 1974), 15.

Radebaugh, B. F. "Student Teachers, Knowledge, and Effective Teaching Behavior." The Journal of Teacher Education, 21 (Summer 1970), 173-177.

Rost, L. "Remember Your Student Teaching." Agricultural Education, 47 (August 1974), 41.

Sinclair, W. and L. K. Peters. "Cooperating Teacher-Student Teacher As A Learning Team." The Clearing House, 44 (March 1970), 430-432.

Stillman, A. C. "To The Student Teacher." Journal of Health, Physical Education, and Recreation, 44 (October 1973), 57.

Swineford, E. J. "Critical Teaching Strategies." The Journal of Teacher Education, 22 (Spring 1971), 29-36.

Walter, J. E. "Classroom Control For Student Teachers." School and Community, 61 (April 1975), 13.

Weber, M. "Internship or Student Teaching." Physical Educator, 33 (May 1976) 74-77.

Weinstock, H. R. and C. M. Peccolo. "Do Students' Ideas and Attitudes Survive Practice Teaching?" <u>The Elementary School Journal</u>, 70 (January 1970), 210-218.

INDEX

OTHER TITLES AVAILABLE FROM
CENTURY TWENTY ONE PUBLISHING

NEW DIRECTIONS IN ETHNIC STUDIES: MINORITIES IN AMERICA by David
    Claerbaut, Editor   Perfect Bound   LC# 80-69327
    ISBN 0-86548-025-7 $9.95
COLLECTING, CULTURING, AND CARING FOR LIVING MATERIALS: GUIDE FOR
    TEACHER, STUDENT AND HOBBYIST by William E. Claflin   Perfect
    Bound   LC# 80-69329   ISBN 0-86548-026-5 $8.50
TEACHING ABOUT THE OTHER AMERICANS: MINORITIES IN UNITED STATES
    HISTORY by Ann Curry   Perfect Bound   LC# 80-69120
    ISBN 0-86548-028-1 $8.95
MULTICULTURAL TRANSACTIONS: A WORKBOOK FOCUSING ON COMMUNICATION
    BETWEEN GROUPS by James S. DeLo and William A. Green   Perfect
    Bound   LC# 80-69328   ISBN 0-86548-030-3 $11.50
LEARNING TO TEACH by Richard B. Dierenfield   Perfect Bound
    LC# 80-69119   ISBN 0-86548-031-1 $10.95
LEARNING TO THINK--TO LEARN by M. Ann Dirkes   Perfect Bound
    LC# 80-65613   ISBN 0-86548-032-X $11.50
PLAY IN PRESCHOOL MAINSTREAMED AND HANDICAPPED SETTINGS by Anne Cairns
    Federlein   Perfect Bound   LC# 80-65612   ISBN 0-86548-035-4
    $10.50
THE NATURE OF LEADERSHIP FOR HISPANICS AND OTHER MINORITIES by
    Ernest Yutze Flores   Perfect Bound   LC# 80-69239
    ISBN 0-86548-036-2 $10.95
THE MINI-GUIDE TO LEADERSHIP by Ernest Yutze Flores   Perfect Bound
    LC# 80-83627   ISBN 0-86548-037-0 $5.50
THOUGHTS, TROUBLES AND THINGS ABOUT READING FROM THE CRADLE THROUGH
    GRADE THREE by Carolyn T. Gracenin   Perfect Bound
    LC# 80-65611   ISBN 0-86548-038-9 $14.95
BETWEEN TWO CULTURES: THE VIETNAMESE IN AMERICA by Alan B. Henkin and
    Liem Thanh Nguyen   Perfect Bound   LC# 80-69333
    ISBN 0-86548-039-7 $7.95
PERSONALITY CHARACTERISTICS AND DISCIPLINARY ATTITUDES OF CHILD-
    ABUSING MOTHERS by Alan L. Evans   Perfect Bound   LC# 80-69240
    ISBN 0-86548-033-8 $11.95
PARENTAL EXPECTATIONS AND ATTITUDES ABOUT CHILDREARING IN HIGH RISK
    VS. LOW RISK CHILD ABUSING FAMILIES by Gary C. Rosenblatt
    Perfect Bound   LC# 79-93294   ISBN 0-86548-020-6 $10.00
CHILD ABUSE AS VIEWED BY SUBURBAN ELEMENTARY SCHOOL TEACHERS by David
    A. Pelcovitz   Perfect Bound   LC# 79-93295   ISBN 0-86548-019-2
    $10.00
PHYSICAL CHILD ABUSE: AN EXPANDED ANALYSIS by James R. Seaberg
    Perfect Bound   LC# 79-93293   ISBN 0-86548-021-4 $10.00
THE DISPOSITION OF REPORTED CHILD ABUSE by Marc F. Maden   Perfect
    Bound   LC# 79-93296   ISBN 0-86548-016-8 $10.00
EDUCATIONAL AND PSYCHOLOGICAL PROBLEMS OF ABUSED CHILDREN by James
    Christiansen   Perfect Bound   LC# 79-93303   ISBN 0-86548-003-6
    $10.00
DEPENDENCY, FRUSTRATION TOLERANCE, AND IMPULSE CONTROL IN CHILD ABUSERS
    by Don Kertzman   Perfect Bound   LC# 79-93297   ISBN 86548-015-X
    $10.00
SUCCESSFUL STUDENT TEACHING: A HANDBOOK FOR ELEMENTARY AND SECONDARY
    STUDENT TEACHERS by Fillmer Hevener, Jr.   Perfect Bound
    LC# 80-69332   ISBN 0-86548-040-0 $8.95
BLACK COMMUNICATION IN WHITE SOCIETY by Roy Cogdell and Sybil Wilson
    Perfect Bound   LC# 79-93302   ISBN 0-86548-004-4 $13.00

SCHOOL VANDALISM: CAUSE AND CURE by Robert Bruce Williams and Joseph
     L. Venturini   Perfect Bound   LC# 80-69230   ISBN 0-86548-060-5
     $9.50
LEADERS, LEADING, AND LEADERSHIP by Harold W. Boles   Perfect Bound
     LC# 80-65616   ISBN 0-86548-023-0 $14.95
LEGAL OUTLOOK: A MESSAGE TO COLLEGE AND UNIVERSITY PEOPLE by Ulysses
     V. Spiva   Perfect Bound   LC# 80-69232   ISBN 0-86548-057-5
     $9.95
THE NAKED CHILD THE LONG RANGE EFFECTS OF FAMILY AND SOCIAL NUDITY
     by Dennis Craig Smith   Perfect Bound   LC# 80-69234
     ISBN 0-86548-056-7 $7.95
SIGNIFICANT INFLUENCE PEOPLE: A SIP OF DISCIPLINE AND ENCOURAGEMENT
     by Joseph C. Rotter, Johnnie McFadden and Gary D. Kannenberg
     Perfect Bound   LC# 80-69233   ISBN 0-86548-055-9 $8.95
LET'S HAVE FUN WITH ENGLISH by Ruth Rackmill   Perfect Bound
     LC# 80-68407   ISBN 0-86548-061-3 $6.95
CHILDREN'S PERCEPTIONS OF ELDERLY PERSONS by Lillian A. Phenice
     Perfect Bound   LC# 80-65604   ISBN 0-86548-054-0 $10.50
URBAN EDUCATION: AN ANNOTATED BIBLIOGRAPHY by Arnold G. Parks
     Perfect Bound   LC# 80-69234   ISBN 0-86548-053-2 $9.50
DYNAMICS OF CLASSROOM STRUCTURE by Charles J. Nier   Perfect Bound
     LC# 80-69330   ISBN 0-86548-052-4 $11.50
SOCIOLOGY IN BONDAGE: AN INTRODUCTION TO GRADUATE STUDY by Harold A.
     Nelson   Perfect Bound   LC# 80-65605   ISBN 0-86548-051-6 $9.95
BEYOND THE OPEN CLASSROOM: TOWARD INFORMAL EDUCATION by Lorraine L.
     Morgan, Vivien C. Richman and Ann Baldwin Taylor   Perfect Bound
     LC# 80-69235   ISBN 0-86548-050-8 $9.50
INTRODUCTORY SOCIOLOGY: LECTURES, READINGS AND EXERCISES by Gordon D.
     Morgan   Perfect Bound   LC# 80-65606   ISBN 0-86548-049-4
     $10.50
THE STUDENT TEACHER ON THE FIRING LINE by D. Eugene Meyer   Perfect
     Bound   LC# 80-69236   ISBN 0-86548-048-6 $11.95
VALUES ORIENTATION IN SCHOOL by Johnnie McFadden and Joseph C. Rotter
     Perfect Bound   LC# 80-69238   ISBN 0-86548-045-1 $4.50
MOVEMENT THEMES: TOPICS FOR EARLY CHILDHOOD LEARNING THROUGH CREATIVE
     MOVEMENT by Barbara Stewart Jones   Perfect Bound   LC# 80-65608
     ISBN 0-86548-042-7 $8.50
FROM BIRTH TO TWELVE: HOW TO BE A SUCCESSFUL PARENT TO INFANTS AND
     CHILDREN by Gary D. Kannenberg   Perfect Bound   LC# 80-69331
     ISBN 0-86548-043-5 $7.95